Passion and partings
the dying sayings
of early Quakers

Jane Mace

First published in great Britain in 2020 by Quacks Books

Copyright © Jane Mace

isbn 978-1-912728-26-8

Published and printed by
Quacks Books
7 Grape Lane
Petergate
York Yo1 7hu
info@quacks.info
www.radiusonline.info
0044 (0)1904 635967

Contents

Cover photograph: Rob Cockbain, *Godwits in flight*
Mersey Estuary Conservation Group (2020)

Foreword

Quaker practice asks a profound question: how do we learn from one another about our spiritual life? Ours is first an experiential awareness of God, the Inner Light, Spirit – we find a 'knowing' in ourselves before we are asked, in a familiar Quaker phrase, But what canst *thou* say? Quakers have always shared this 'knowing', through ministry in Meeting, travel, writing and publishing, even minute-writing in business meetings.

More formal processes – courses, study groups and residential gatherings – have developed in recent decades, but the intention is always to share true exploration and discovery rather than to formalize and make credal our deepest spiritual experiences. I thought I was familiar with all these processes until I was invited to write this foreword.

In her sensitive research into a less well-known practice of early Quakers, Jane Mace does a great service to both our inner and outer ways of learning. I had never before been aware of the publication of 'dying sayings' in which scribes took notes of the parting words of Quakers, later making a fair copy so that others might read these testimonies to faithful lives and to their trust in divine grace as they departed this world. Her work provides a wonderful insight, not only to the practice itself, but to the way the texts can speak to a contemporary reader. There is no doubt that in reading, we have to listen carefully to 'where the words come from': the 1700s were a time when Biblical, Christian language was the norm for Quakers, and at first this can seem to some of us oppressively narrow. Then we begin to be drawn into these lives – those who suffered bitterly for their faith, being imprisoned and persecuted, giving up lucrative trade for their conscience's sake, or who endured the privations of illness with limited palliative care. They range widely in age and circumstance, but all, with their scribes and editors, hold to the sense of mission felt by early Quakers: 'They had found a truth and they wanted others to learn from this finding.'

Jane Mace offers us a scholar's analysis of the sayings, their context and their publication. As importantly, she records the trajectory of her own responses: from confusion and resistance because of the unfamiliar phrasing and language, to love and connection with those 'who are part of the family history of today's Religious Society of Friends, and who laid the ground for us to grow in.'

I begin, in reading, to feel the same connection with those who are about to enter the great silence of death and who are enabled to share their experience of a faithful life with others. Passion is a word not often associated with quiet, restrained, orderly Quakers; and yet it blazes through these guides - ' not so much about death and dying as about life and living' - illuminating both their world and ours, challenging us to think again about how and when our lives speak, and to what purpose.

Jennifer Barraclough
Director
Woodbrooke Quaker Study Centre (1999-2010)

July 2020

INTRODUCTION

There is no oral history of early Quakers and their firsthand experience. Their lives have been researched and reported by others or written as memoirs, but for a religion committed to listening to speech rather than reading text, it feels a shame that there is no chance to hear how their words would have been spoken. This was a movement whose founders travelled and preached from one part of England to many parts of the world. What might their voices have sounded like?

It has been exciting to find one source to help imagine them: a series of tracts based on the spoken words of the founding Friends, originally recorded in their last days or hours, even on their deathbeds. This book provides a sample of these tracts, first published over three centuries ago, bound in a leatherbound volume of octavo pages.

It is hard to know how many copies of this particular volume might still be in existence. Let us say one for each national Quaker library, and more still lurking in the archives and libraries of local Quaker Meetings across Britain and beyond. That would mean that somewhere, there might be several hundred copies of it (and of the others in the collection).

The copy I have been working from has just two words on its spine: 'Piety promoted'. Only once inside is the full title revealed:

Piety Promoted,
IN A
COLLECTION
OF THE
Dying Sayings
Of many of the
People call'd Quakers,
WITH
A Brief Account of some of their
Labours in the GOSPEL, and
Sufferings for the same

————————

By John Tomkins

————————————————

London, Printed and Sold by
T.*Sowle* in
White-Hart-court in *Gracious-Street,*
1703

To me it has felt a unique object, hitherto unread by anyone else. But of course in reality, many hands must have turned its pages before mine; discovering inside a series of portraits, mixing inspirations and warnings with mini-biographies. Each is introduced by an editor who is also a kind of reporter: offering, as the title promises, 'brief accounts' of the individual's life – and some version of their sayings.

The volume contains three Parts; and in each Part, some fifty such accounts. My first skim through these took place when, in September 2018, I borrowed the book for the first time from our Area Meeting archives and took it home. Within an hour, I was engrossed. Within a month, I had taken it to Friends House library in London to learn more. David Irwin, librarian, took a look at it. "This is one of many other volumes in the collection here", he told me – "a total of nine or ten in all. There is a full set here", he said, "so this one is for your Meeting to keep safe."

"Printed of course by Tace Sowle", he went on, "an important Quaker printer of the time; inheriting her father's business". (Ah. What a difference a name makes. Having only seen 'T.Sowle' identified in the flyleaf I had had no idea of the printer's gender.)

I went home and made a first attempt to write a short introduction to it; thinking it might be of use to local Friends – and eventually, the county archive where the rest of our older records live - and returned it to our library. Other commitments took over, more months passed. Then, with late summer coming on, I remembered it; felt I owed some more research for our AM records, began online catalogue searches and returned to the shelves of Friends House and Woodbrooke Quaker Study Centre libraries in London and Birmingham. Over the following weeks questions began to sprout like seedlings.

1. What concept of 'piety' runs through the 'sayings'?
2. Who wrote them? as first-person speech, who served as scribes?
3. How did their authors get chosen? (in age, they range between 9 and 90 years old; in location, they are from all parts of England, Scotland, Ireland, Wales, North America and Barbados);
4. How did the writing get distributed - and with what Quaker authority?
5. What can we learn from the way they would have been read? and
6. What was their wider context?

This book is the result of answers found over several more months, encompassing dark winter days and the very much stranger sunshine months of a world pandemic. In these conditions my inner teacher gave me an urgency to get it shaped and completed.

The chapters that follow include a scatter of reflections on that experience: that of one 21st century Quaker reading the recorded 'dying sayings' of around a hundred others, from another time. The research has no claim to be a careful academic study on an equal footing with more scholarly work. Rather it has felt like a conversation with people long gone, to whom I have come to recognise that I belong and have developed an obligation.

That conversation has revealed two things.
1. While listed as 'dying sayings', these texts are intended to offer not so much a set of guides about death and dying as about life and living. The whole

enterprise of collecting 'last words' had grown from the sense of mission felt by early Quakers. They had found a truth and they wanted others to learn from that finding.

2. Secondly, while the heading implies a series of quotes from individuals on their deathbeds, it has actually included the sayings of others, witnesses to these last moments: the friends and relatives who visited and conversed with them, their scribes, who captured the words on paper, and their editors.

Containing the *spoken* words of their subjects, they are more like interviews than obituaries, let alone memoirs: and as their readers, you and I join their listeners present at their bedsides.

The speakers are a mix. Some, at the time, would have been well known as key figures in the early stages of their radical movement. Many others would have been known to their local community of Friends, but no further. The names of nearly all of them (listed in the index) would be entirely strange to today's Quakers; yet they are part of the family history of our Religious Society of Friends. Their discoveries and journeys, their sufferings and determination laid the ground for us to grow in.

The commitment also represented by 'their dying sayings' is inspiring: a commitment by publishers, editors and speakers to *pass on a message* – that a frightening and painful death can also, with the help of the divine within us all, be happy. Life today in pandemic times with the daily news of national and global death tolls has, for many, made dying an abstract and numerical matter, but for many others, shockingly close and real. These accounts of other deaths in the past, often with exchanges between the dying and a close group of witnesses, gives another perspective.

The book that they have given me to write has been through several phases and shapes before it arrived at the one in your hands. At first I had thought the most useful thing I might do would be to present, unadorned and complete, a selection of the original 'sayings'. However, many of these contain the repetitions which would be expected from a spoken text – but appear laborious on the page. Instead, each of the chapters that follow contains a few of the 'sayings' at a time (with cuts to the lengthier ones). In order to help have a sense of each of the speakers, I have indicated (as far as these were made clear in the original) the year of their death, their age when they died, and their location.

At the end of each, I have offered a reflective note to suggest context and themes - as follows:
1: ways and means of reading, then and now;
2: the production and publication of Quaker writing;
3: some of the persecutions suffered by early Quakers;
4: interpretations and understandings of 'piety';
5: partings - for the mourners and the dying; and
6: the Quaker message and meanings then and now.

By way of conclusion, Appendix 3 contains an account of the total 'collection', together with detail of its editors, purposes and printers.

Of all the phrases that first drew me to the faith and practice of Quakers these continue to hold me:

> As a *'community of seekers'*, what we seek, in our worship, is *'a gathered stillness'*. Despite ourselves, we are committed to being *'open to new learning'*, Through a habit of listening, humbly and with passion, we know that there is a strength and joy to be found from *'that of God'* within each one of us – including ourselves.

This was the gist of the original Quaker message that remains with us today. From their world of turbulence and confusion, the early Quakers teach us, in ours, how every one of us has the power to find, as well as to seek.

In my case, I found this volume by accident. I had no idea of its subjects becoming my companions in another search. But that is one of the strange gifts that God sometimes offers.

Acknowledgements

My thanks are due to the trustees of Sessions Book Trust, York for their support in the costs of this book's publication; to the libraries of Woodbrooke Quaker Centre and Friends House for their invaluable archives; to Friends past and present - particularly those of Gloucestershire Area Meeting (including my husband, John Geale) - for lively conversations and encouragement; and to staff at 'The Friend' for their continuing commitment to high quality weekly publishing through hard times.

Jane Mace, August 2020

A note on dates

*Early Friends preferred to call months 'the first Month',
'the second Month' rather than using month names. They
also preferred a numerical indicator for days of the week:
using First day, Second day, and so on – instead of Monday
and Tuesday.*

*In reading these accounts, we need to be aware of another
more general difference between the calendar at the time
and the one in use today, not special to Quakers.*

*Until 1752, England had hung on to the usage of 'Lady
Day' (25ᵗʰ March) as being the first day of the calendar year:
New Year's day. By then, most other European countries
had changed to the Gregorian calendar - with 1ˢᵗ January as
the beginning of the year. England had taken a while to
catch up.*

*So at the time of 'Piety Promoted' publications, the English
calendar was still the mediaeval one. (This means, for
example, that when we read of someone dying in the 2nd
Month, we should think of them as ending their life, not in
February, but in April.)*

1 SAYINGS

The introduction to Part I of the volume opens in personal terms:

> To the READER. I here present thee with a Collection of the Dying Sayings of some Persons, who Lived and Died in Faith and Communion with the People of God called *Quakers.*

There follows a long recital, including several biblical references in the margin, of the good lives led by these 'persons' whom God had been 'pleased to call forth into that Work' and so supported them as to give them 'full Assurance of Eternal Life in the World to come.'

In contrast to this opening, the conclusion then reads as an address to a public gathering:

> 'The Lord give them that read, a Heart to understand the Things which belong to their Peace; and if these be any means to stir up any to more Faithfulness and Diligence, in making their Calling and Election sure, my Design is answered, and God shall have the praise of all, who is worthy for ever'.

The sayings and their extracts that I have chosen to offer here cannot be the originals as their first readers met them. Here they are printed in a very different font on larger pages than the little octavo sheets of their first printing. In addition, I have inserted paragraph spaces to help the present-day reader – and made some cuts to the text for space reasons

1

(indicated by these dots ....) In copying from the original, whenever I was uncertain of a word or phrase, I have added **(sic)**[1] beside it.

With one exception, I have kept the uses of **capital letters, punctuation, italics** and **spelling** of the original texts. (The exception is the saying of Deborah Bell in Chapter 5. There is a reason for this, which I explain there.)

Before meeting these Friends, it feels important to remember two things. First, that these texts - or at least the quotations within them - were originally *spoken* words; and that Friends who read them at the time would often be *hearing them read aloud* – very possibly in a gathered meeting.   And second, that these were published for a contemporary audience, with shared knowledge both of scripture and often of the living circumstances of the authors.

With no more comment, I now leave you to meet four Friends, almost as if you were joining them in a Quaker meeting: introducing them here by their names, dates, ages at death, and geography. After their 'ministries' we will regather (as in a meeting for worship) for some reflection.

Elizabeth Furley	1656-1669 (13)	Colchester
Christopher Bacon	1623-1678 (55)	Somersetshire
Alice Curwen	1619-1679 (60)	Lancashire
Mary Harris	1633-1668 (35)	London

---

[1] (Sic) is the word commonly used in brackets after a copied or quoted word that appears odd or wrong: to show that the word is quoted exactly as it stands in the original,.

2

Elizabeth Furley, Daughter of *John Furley of Colchester*, was a Child that loved the Lord, and also those that feared him; her delight was to hear Truth preach'd, and to be with such who excell'd in Vertue, feared and hated a Lye; and lived and died in the Faith which the People call'd *Quakers* do profess.

She was taken sick at her Father's House in *Colchester*, the 11th of the 12th Month, 1669. Two days before she died, being fill'd with the Love of God, she utter'd many precious Sayings, concerning the Lord, and his Mercies towards her; praying to the Lord, that she might be faithful to the end. And in the presence of several Persons, spoke as followeth (with more, which for Brevity's sake is omitted, that was taken down in Characters)

Whatever is not of thy self, Lord, purge it out of me; yea, purge me thoroughly, leave no wicked word in me: Thrust away the Power of Darkness, Lord, make me able to praise thee. Let me not come into that way which is evil; for if I do, I shall dishonour thee, and thy Truth: I hope I shall never rebel against thee more, but have full satisfaction in thee, and in thy ways, and not in the evil one, and his ways. Wash me, O Lord, thoroughly; let not an unadvised word come out of my Mouth: With more to the same purport. – *Shew them O Lord, the evil of their ways, that have done evilly; and lay a Burden upon their Spirits, that they may leave it. I feel no pain; the Lord is good to me; good is the Will of the Lord; let thy Will be done in Earth, as it is done in Heaven: Everlasting Kindness hast thou shewn me, and I hope I shall never forget it, while I am in this World.*

With more, in admiration of the Kindness and Mercies of God, and her desire to serve him whilst she lived. And to one of her brothers, she said, *Improve thy time, for thou knowest not how soon thou may'st be taken away;* warning him of the dangers of an Evil Life; and took him about the neck, and kissed him, saying, *Mind what I say, O dear brother:* with many more words she exhorted him.

She also admonished her other Brothers with *tender Expressions, saying, Love the Lord, Brothers; Love good Men; hate the Devil; but Oh Love the Lord, and then you will be a Joy to your Father and Mother.*

When she saw one of her Sisters weep, she said *Weep not for me, I am very well. – All serve the Lord, that he may be your Portion: in my Father's house there is Bread enough, there is fulness, want of nothing; yea, there is fulness of Bread, durable Riches, and Honour; I desire never to forget the Lord.*

As she walk'd in Innocency, she dy'd in Peace, and enter'd into Glory, the 16th Day of the 12th Month, 1669. Aged 13 years and 5 weeks.

Christopher Bacon, on *Polling-Hill,* in *Somersetshire,* was formerly a Soldier in the King's Army; About the year 1656, some of the Lord's Servants, called *Quakers,* coming into that Country to Preach the Gospel, the said *Christopher* went to one of the Meetings, *not to receive Good, but rather to Scoff and Deride;*

but, thro' the Lord's Mercy, he was reach'd in his Conscience, and received the blessed Truth, in the Love of it; and afterwards received a Dispensation of the Gospel of Christ to Preach, and was a diligent Labourer in the Work of the Ministry; and travelled to *London,* and into *Ireland* and *Wales,* and many parts of the Nation of *England,* and several were convinced of Truth by him;

And coming into the County of *Cornwall,* in the year 1678, he fell Sick, being weak of Body before, he had a good Meeting with Friends in the Town: and upon his Sick-Bed, desired a Friend by him to write comfortably to his Wife, if the Lord shou'd take him away, and advise, *That she bring up his Children in the Fear and Counsel of the Lord; and it was his fervent desire, that his Wife might be kept to Truth, and for all Friends.* And said,

Since it is my lot, after many great Labours and Travels for the Service of Truth, for me to come here, and lay down my Body, I am well satisfied in God's Will and Pleasure, and am at this time free and clear in my mind, willing to be with God. Then making some Pulse (sic), said, *Oh! Friends keep in mind your latter end, and that will make you draw nigh to the Lord, and seek after him.* And further said, *Friends, take heed that you lose not an Heavenly Inheritance for an Earthly.*

And the Day before he dyed, being the first Day of the Week, he spoke to Friends, as they were going to Meeting, minding his dear Love to Friends, and said,

The Lord's Presence be amongst you, for his Presence hath attended me in all my Labours, Travels, Sufferings, and Exercises, for his Name sake.

His End drawing near, and his Body weak, but *continued to the last Moment in sweet Harmony, and lifting up his hands,* and in much Quietness and Peace he gave up the Ghost, the 29th of the 10th Month, 1678. Aged about 55 years.

Alice Curwen of Lancashire, who with her Husband, Thomas Curwen, did Travel in the Work of the Ministry, in divers parts of *America,* as *New-England, New-York, Long-Island, Rhoad-Island, Barbadoes;* and after many long Journeys, and much Service, returned home about the 3rd Month, 1677.

And the said Alice, being Upon her dying bed, was asked, If she thought she should recover her Sickness? Did answer,

> *I do not know what the Lord has to do; but I am freely given up to his Will, whether it be Life or Death; I am as Clear as a Child.*

Another time, complaining of the Unfaithfulness of some Professing Truth, said,

> *But those who are Faithful, the Lord will preserve them, tho' they meet with many Trials and Besetments (sic) both inwardly and outwardly....*

She often, in the time of her Sickness, made Melody to God in her Heart, and said,

> *Oh! My heavenly Father, how hast thou filled my Cup, and made it to overflow; for I can do no less than Bless and Praise thy Eternal Name.*

Desiring often, *God's Will might be done, whether it was Life or Death; for to me, to live is Christ and to dye is Gain.* She exhorted Friends *to be diligent, and to know Life and Vertue in themselves;* for she said, *The Time will come, that Words shall cease, and Life shall more arise;* and said, *If she did live, she must declare it; and if she did dye, she must leave it as a Testimony for the Lord.*

Towards the latter end of the last Night she lived, her Pain was Great, and she spake to Friends about her, saying,

7

Pray to the Lord for me, That he lay no more upon me, than I am able to bear; that I may not offend this good God.

And immediately she prayed to the Lord, and had a little Ease, and lay still, as if she had been in a Slumber, and so grew weaker, and was sweetly carried thro' to the End.

She dyed in *London*, in the year 1680

Historical note

For more about Alice's life, there is this[2]:
She grew up in Cumbria. Her husband was imprisoned several times for tithe refusal. Once their children were grown up, she followed a leading to travel in the ministry to Boston (having heard of the Quaker sufferings there) and beyond. She too was imprisoned and also stocked and whipped on more than one occasion. Her autobiography and correspondence was published in 1680 as 'A Relation of the Labour, Travail and Suffering of that Faithful Servant of the Lord, Alice Curwen'.

(For a note on the experience of early Quakers' experience in Barbados please see Appendix 1)

---

[2] from: Booy (2004) p108-112

Mary Harris, a Maid, Young and Beautiful, that went often with her Relations to the Meetings of the People of God call'd Quakers, and had a Love rais'd in her to the blessed Truth, and to them who held it in a pure Conscience; but still liv'd in the Customs and Fashions of this Evil World;

but the same Love of God that had begotten Tenderness in her Heart, and Love to Truth, followed her, and would not suffer her to sit down in the World, without Trouble, and the Lord visited her with great weakness, and she grew Ill, and fell into a Consumption for about three Years;

and being often visited by Josiah Coale, and put in Mind to consider whether the Hand of the Lord was not upon her for her Unfaithfulness and Disobedience; she did consider the matter, and the Lord set it upon her Heart, and *she cryed to him for Mercy,* and apply'd her Heart to the Lord, and his faithful Messengers, saying,

> *I have hardened my Heart at many precious Meetings, when the Lord hath smitten me; and I have seen plainly, that the Lord would have gathered me; but I said in my Heart, if I receive this, if I give up to this, I must be a Quaker, and I cannot be a Quaker. Then would I take my Heart from attending upon the Ministration of Truth, and then my Heart became more Hard:* What shall I do *(said she)* that now I may receive the Faithful Sayings of the Servants of the Lord? Oh! That my Heart were open; but it is shut and hard; When shall I find Mercy in this state?*

She remained so for some time, and grew weaker and weaker in Body; and on the first day she took her Bed, she was much under the Righteous Judgements of the Lord, and felt his Word in her Heart as Fire; but the Lord in Judgment remembered Mercy, and having brought her very low, he shew'd her the Child's State, which she with great Delight desired; and indeed she became *as a little Child, fit for the Kingdom of Heaven;* then did the Lord rend the Veil, and shew'd her his Glory, and the Preciousness of his pure Truth; and the Light shined out of Darkness, and in it she saw Light, and received the Knowledge of God; and her Heart was fill'd with Joy and Praises to the Lord, saying,

> *I am Well; I feel no Pain; I am full; my Cup runs over; I am filled, as it were, with Marrow and Fatness; I have seen his Glory,and tasted his precious Truth. How Pure is God's Everlasting Truth? Nothing so Pure; and they who indeed receive it, are made Pure by it: Praised be the Lord, who hath made me Partaker of it, and placed me among his People: Oh! Blessed God, who hath given me Cause to Sing aloud of thy Praise:*

With many precious words, speaking to several Persons who came to visit her, to their several Conditions; shewing to some, who lived in Pleasure, her Hands, saying,

> *See here, the Lord hath made these Bones bare for my Rebellion, because I would not submit to his precious Truth; he hath brought me to the Dust, and I must lay down this Body as a Sacrifice; Oh! Don't you stand out, it will cost you dear, if ever you find Mercy....*

More sensible Expressions she uttered, which I omit for Brevity; and about half an Hour before her Departure, she was taken with very great Trembling, and seemed to be somewhat troubled, one near her said, What is the matter? Art thou in any doubt concerning the Truth of which thou art made Partaker? She replied,

> *No, no, that's God's pure everlasting Truth, which the People of God, called Quakers, are made Partakers of, and for which they Suffer; that is Everlasting, that is the true Spirit, and their God is my God; and altho' I see it not now as I have seen it, yet I bring in my Testimony, That is the Truth that shall abide for ever... .*

Then she breathed a little thicker about the space of a quarter of an Hour, and without Groan or Sigh, or the least Motion, she shut her Eyes, and Slept. Glory to God for Ever. She dyed at the Widow *Mary Forster's,* in that called *St John's Street,* near *Smith-Field, London, 1668.*

Reflection

Elizabeth Furley, the youngest of this group, is saying a prayer in her dying hours, asking God to receive her; and then, asking her brothers and sisters to 'mind what she says'. Christopher Bacon is shown as transformed from sceptic to convert, adopting a life committed to serve as a missionary for the faith he had once scorned and urging his listeners to follow his example.

Alice Curwen, the only published writer of the group, is giving herself up to God's will after a life of long journeys and much service. From the historical note we also learn of the extreme persecution she endured in the ministry.
Mary Harris was in a quandary about her convincement, but once decided, like Christopher Bacon, she is transformed by meeting the 'people of God call'd Quakers' and has the most to say at her end-of-life moments.

In each case present-day readers are as much their audience as those at their bedside, meeting each of them through the filter of another listener: the editor of the collection, sometimes (but not always) the same person as the scribe at their side, recording their words.

There are many ways of reading. In everyday twenty-first century life print is all around us. We catch it in quick glances, almost out of the corner of the eye. In the search for the gist of something, skimming print is routine. On screens, readers expect to scroll through whole paragraphs without a pause. We tend to read fast.

By contrast, my first reading of the original 'sayings' required time. The vocabulary was unfamiliar; the pages small; the style of punctuation and spelling foreign; above all, the content felt intense, abstract and sometimes disturbing. Because my own religious faith is not used to referring to the divine as 'the Lord', there was an obstacle for me to overcome. It just took time (and humility) to overcome it; slowing down my usual speed and rereading the texts more than once.

More on reading

By the 1640s and 50s it would have been generally assumed that reading, whether chapbooks, broadsides or religious tracts such as those published by Friends, was a shared activity. A range of 'small books and pleasant histories' would have offered other sorts of reading[3] including 'small merry books' and 'small godly books' among them. The pedlar of print 'could be a messenger bearing God's word into towns and villages across the country', with ballad sellers usually trading at fairs[4].

In her work on 'cheap print and popular piety', Tessa Watt argues that spoken and written cultures of the time were 'intrinsically linked', with the printed word routinely being read or sung aloud; sung ballads pinned up on walls for decoration'. She reports that the first Quaker print runs of the period were quite small – 100 copies at a time. By 1656, however, Friends had decided that 600 copies of every Quaker book published should be printed, allowing copies to be sent directly as a matter of course to local meetings.

---

[3] Spufford (1981)
[4] Watt, p244

As I have said, I do not know how many copies of the various volumes of 'Dying Sayings' were published. But I fondly believe there is a Quaker record somewhere that could tell us.

God's voice

To early Quakers, it seems that true ministry, whether spoken or written, was a direct and authentic utterance from God. In Edward Burrough's words:

> 'I write not as from man... but as from the eternal and spiritual light....For who Speaks, Writes, or Declares from the light of God.... Speaks, Writes, and Declares not as from man... but as from God, whose light is spiritual... and from this light did the Prophets and Ministers of God...Speak, Write and Declare.'[5]

For Friends, there was equal merit in both spoken and written words, because they argued that

> 'the holy spirit which had moved men to write the scriptures was also present in them; and that consequently their utterances – spoken or written – were as valid as those of the apostles.'

There seems to have been – and may still be - a Quaker equation between preaching and publishing. But preachers had the advantage over authors, being in a better position to control interpretation - and so, as Kathleen Peters points out, able to respond to audience reaction more immediately than they could achieve with their written texts.[6]

---

[5] Edward Burrough, 1654, quoted in Peters (2005) p21
[6] Peters (2005) p29-30

The practice of collecting 'dying sayings of a people called Quakers' published between 1701 and 1810 resulted in some four hundred and fifty-five such pieces being published, in the form of nine volumes. (There is more detail in Appendix 3)

All were edited in various ways by those who 'collected' their words. All were intended to inspire.

2 AUTHORSHIP

How did these 'dying sayings' fit in with other published writing of the time? I find it helpful to remember that the Quaker movement began only a few decades after printed writing had become generally available. Once print was around it would have still been some time before those who were able to read did so on their own, silently. As one historian memorably wrote, until the end of the 19th century,

> 'most printed words found their way into the minds of most of the populations...through their ears rather than their eyes.'[1]

When Quakers began publishing, then, they must have expected words to be heard as much as seen. In the early days, with the growing number of 'Friends of Truth' meeting together, epistles were being sent in some numbers from Swarthmoor Hall in Cumbria (the movement's main distribution centre) and read aloud - along with autobiographies, prophesies, sermons, reports of the persecution and sufferings endured. By the time the first 'Dying Sayings' tracts appeared in the early 1700s, they were in good company.

At that stage, Friends who were published authors in the conventional sense were, relatively speaking, a minority. At the same time, they produced a lot of work. Of the estimated 40,000 people by 1660 gathering to join the 'Friends of Truth' (growing in number until the 1680s) just a hundred or so were authors of printed tracts. (They still

---

[1] Vincent (2000) p94

managed to produce some three hundred titles, many going into several editions). As Kathleen Peters puts it: 'writing, while essential to the work of travelling ministry, 'was not an inherent part of being a Quaker'[2]. The reading out of a published Quaker text, indoors or outdoors[3], would have gone on as part of a still generally oral culture.

Each dying saying account contains a mix of introduction and narrative along with the quoted words of the dying person. Those quotations are the nearest we have to the authentic voice of the Friend named (sometimes accompanied by extracts from a letter of theirs). Taking down the spoken words as heard or dictated, their scribe and/or editor may have missed some, or added a few others here and there, but it is the dying Friend who is named as primary author, not the editor.

So from now on, I refer to the named Friend being presented as 'author' and when there is third person narrative I refer to its writer as 'editor'. As it happens, three of the four Friends I have chosen to come next happened to be among those who were published authors in the usual sense. Here, however, the focus is on producing writing from their spoken words and the role played by others in enabling that to happen.

Elizabeth Braithwait	1667-1686 (17)	Kendal
Stephen Crisp	1648-1692 (64)	Colchester
Priscilla Cotton	(?) -1664	Plymouth
George Fox	1624-1690 (66)	Leicester

---

[2] Peters (2005) p8
[3] Watt (1995) p67

Elizabeth Braithwait, a young Maid of seventeen Years of Age, who died in Prison for the Testimony of a good Conscience, at Kendal in Westmoreland - From a Child, God by his Grace did incline her Heart to love, fear, and serve him; and was truly obedient to her Parents, sober and chaste in her Life and Conversation, kind to all, and of a meek and quiet Spirit.

She was, with several others of the people call'd *Quakers*, taken up by a Warrant dated the 25th of the 5th month, 1684 for not going to *Church* (so called) and carry'd to *Kendal* Gaol; after some time she had liberty a few days to be at her Brother's House; but Complaint being made against the Keeper, she was sent for, and she was not easie till she return'd to Prison; for said she, *That is my place, and my present home; there I have most Peace and Content.*

About two Months after her commitment, *viz.* the 17th of the 7th Month, she was taken sick in Prison; her Mother coming to visit her, asked her, if she had a mind to be at home? She reply'd,

> *No, no; I am at home in my place, to my full content; and if my God so order it, that I be dissolved, I had rather dye here, than in any other place; and I am glad that I got to this place before I begun to be sick; here I have Peace and true Content in the Will of God, whether Life or Death; I am only grieved, that there should be so little Tenderness or Pity in the Hearts of my Persecutors, to keep such a poor young one, as I am, in Prison, the Lord forgive them, I can freely.*

And further said, that her

> *Imprisonment was by the Permission of the Almighty, who is greater, and above the greatest of my Persecutors, whom I believe will shortly set me free from these, and all other Bonds, over all their heads; and in his Peace, in true Patience, I possess my Soul, and am contented, if it be his Will, to be dissolved.*

A Friend asked her, why she was so willing to dye? *Oh,* said she, *I have seen Glorious Sights of good things.* The Friend query'd what things? She answer'd, *They are so Excellent and Glorious, that it's not utterable; and now I have nothing but Love and Goodwill to all:* But more especially she was glad *in the Love and Unity that she felt with Friends;* with whom, said she, *I have been often Refreshed in our Meetings together, with the Refreshment that comes from the Presence of the Lord: Oh! The good Evening Meetings that we have had.*

Another time, she said to her Mother,

> *They say, that we shall spend all our Riches with lying here in Prison: Nay, our Riches are durable, and our Treasure hidden, laid up in Heaven.*

Her Mother, feeling her lie under great weight of Sickness, would sometime Weep: she would be always troubled at it and say,

> *Dear Mother, do not weep, but resign me freely up into the Hands of the Lord; weep not for me, for I am well, Christ my Redeemer is with me.* And to her Sister, she said, *Come Sister, lie down by me,*

do not sorrow for me, I am well content to Live or Dye; for my God hath Blessed me, and will Bless me, and his Blessing rests upon me.

And a little before she departed, her Speech fail'd; after which she would sing in her Heart, lifting up her Hands, with a Chearful (sic) Countenance, and taking her Friends by the hand, with great Affection; and so fell asleep in the Lord, 28th of the 7th Month, 1684 in the 17th Year of her Age.

Historical note

Elizabeth was one of many. Quaker historian Richard Allen notes the brutal statistics: 'As many as 450 Quakers died in prison during Charles II's reign...[4] Conditions in prisons were extremely grim as they were usually dimly lit, poorly ventilated, and inmates were forced to sleep on cold floors or wet straw. Friends were often abused by over-zealous gaolers or fellow inmates....'

He goes on to observe that, like Elizabeth Braithwait, 'Friends were most likely to be prosecuted in the civil courts for not attending church services.[5]

---

[4] (1660-1685)
[5] Allen (2013) p32

Stephen Crisp of Colchester in Essex, received the blessed Truth about the Year 1655 when he was about 27 Years of Age, and was a Preacher of the Everlasting Gospel of Christ Jesus for about 35 Years, and in that Service he travell'd in many parts of *England, Scotland, Holland, Germany,* and the *Low Countries*...and endured many Hardships for his faithful Testimony to the blessed Truth. He was greatly capable, through his long Experience, to Advise and give Counsel to Persons in all Conditions.

In the later part of his days, unable to travel much, through indisposition of Body, yet diligent in *Preaching the Gospel in Colchester and London*....and about four Days before he Died, being under much Bodily Weakness and Pain, *G.Whitehead* visiting him, S.C. said, ***I see an end of Mortality yet cannot come at it. I desire the Lord to deliver me out of this Troublesome and Painful body; if he will but say his Word it is done. Yet there is noe Cloud in my way. I have a full assurance of my Peace with God in Christ Jesus. My integrity and Uprightness of Heart is known in Jesus Christ who made me see this is Upright to God.*** Dear George, I can live and dye with thee and my dear love is with thee and to all the Faithful in the Church of God.'

And remember'd his Love to all the *Faithful in the Church of God.*. And to another Friend, he said, *I have fought the good Fight of Faith, and have run my Course, and am waiting for the Crown of Life, that is laid up for me.* And to another Friend, visiting him, he said, *Serve the Truth, for the simple Truth's sake, and it will preserve thee to the end, as it hath done me.*

And in his great pain of Body, feeling the Word of Patience to support him, he said to the Friends watching with him, *Grow in the Word of Patience, that it may keep you also in the time of need.* And the day before he died, S.C, said *I hope I am gathering* (as his Expression was understood) *I hope, I hope;* being then hardly able to speak out his words; G.W. near parting from him said, *Dear Stephen, would'st thou have anything to Friends?*

After some pause, he gave this answer:
Remember my dear Love in Christ Jesus to all.
And on the 28th Day of the 6th Month, 1692, died in the Lord, at *Wansworth, near London* at 64th Year of his Age.

Historical note

In this Saying the words in **bold italic** were scribed by George Whitehead from Stephen Crisp's words to him and quoted in the minutes of the 'Second Day Morning Meeting' when it met the same year.

This was the committee which, set up twenty years earlier, had the responsibility for any publishing under the name of the Society.[6] Their task, Betty Hagglund tells us, was to check all the manuscripts they received, supervise and (if felt necessary) censor their printing – even 'deciding line by line which passages were to be altered or omitted'[7] Only with their approval could any be published.

---

[6] Hagglund (2013) p481
[7] ibid p483

23

This gives an impression of a committee focussed on amending, cutting or rejecting contributions. From the example of Stephen Crisp's text, however, it seems that sometimes they took a more active editorial approach, interested in helping a text to grow rather than be cut, allowing extra snatches of dialogue with other witnesses at the bedside to be added to the first words recorded.

Stephen Crisp would have been well known to those present (not least, perhaps, for his 32 published sermons [8] and numerous Epistles) but their minute, following the note of what they had already heard, records their wish for more about him from those present – and what they had decided to do about it:

> 'Benjamin Bealing is desired to enter this in his Book and also that William Crouch be spoken with, that the rest of the Remarkable Expressions spoken by Steven Crisp on his Dying Bed that can be perfectly Rembered (sic) be brought in – Samuel Walderfield and John Field to speak to William Crouch thereof.'

The whole account we have just read was the resulting, expanded text that later appeared in the 'Piety Promoted' volume. Containing as it does three additional sayings of his ('to another friend', 'to another friend' and to 'G.W.') recalled by others, it offers an extra flavour of their affection for him: their beloved Friend, remembering his love for others and care for his meeting even in his last hour.

---

[8] Graves (2013) p.280

Priscilla Cotton, formerly Wife of *Arthur Cotton,* who then dwelt in *Plymouth* in *Cornwall,* now of *Colchester* in *Essex*...lived an honourable Life, and was valiant for Truth, and often bore public Testimony to it in Steeple-Houses, and other Places, against the Priests and Professors, who walked out of the Truth, and for her Testimony she suffered several Imprisonments, and Cruel Dealings from them, and other Instruments imploy'd by them.

Moreover she Travelled in several Places, bearing Testimony for Truth in the Living Power of God. She also in her Life time gave forth several good Papers, which are Printed; and lastly, the Day she died, she left a Paper for Friends, as a Testimony of her good will and Love to them all.

After this, seeing her Departure was nigh at hand, she desired several Friends to be called; being come, she desired to be lifted up in her Bed; and in a sense of Life she spake suitably to every one for some time, *Exhorting Friends to Peace and Unity, and to keep in the Cross, which is the power of God, that all might witness a Mortification to Sign, and a Renewedness* (sic) *to Life, that the Living God and his Holy Truth might be Honoured by all; and that Friends might keep out of the Fashions and Customs of the World, both in Words and Apparel, every one answering the Truth therein.*

After this, called for her Husband, who was at that time Weak, Imbracing him, she said
> *My dear Husband, the Lord hath largely Manifested his Love to us, and large has been our Experience thereof, ever since he brought us together to this*

Day; and now my Dear the Lord will separate us, but grieve not, let thy Eye and Expectation be to Him, and the Lord, who hath hitherto helped us, will be thy Help and Support, in whom let thy Trust be for ever!

In like manner she called for her Daughter, and *gave her Charge to live in Subjection to God's Truth, and to forsake what she was convinced of to be Sin and Evil. Saying, if she feared the Lord, and walked in his Truth, it shall be well with Her; but if not, thou wilt be Miserable* and She also spake to other Friends and Relations, which for Brevity is omitted.

Afterwards She said, *Let me lye down that I may Dye*, so in great Stilness and Quietness She departed this Life, about four hours after She had spoken these Words, the fourth Day of the sixth Month, 1664.

Historical note

Among Priscilla Cotton's 'good papers' was a pamphlet that she co-authored with her friend Mary Cole, published in 1655, addressed 'To the Priests and people of England' written while the two were imprisoned together in Exeter for speaking in church.
In it, they argue that the belief that women should be punished in this way, was one based on a misreading of the Bible. Anyone not so inspired, so they argued – including the church ministers who had had them arrested and then

come to visit them in their cell and been reduced to 'filthy speeches' in their fury at the women - should not be speaking at all.

This was her reply to them:[9]

"Now to you all I speak, sin not against the light in your own consciences, be not wilfully blind, but hearken to the light of Jesus Christ in your consciences....

Therefore know you, that you may be, and are ignorant, though you think yourselves wise. Silly men and women may see more into the mystery of Christ Jesus than you.

For the apostles, that the scribes called illiterate [Peter and John; see Acts 4:13] and Mary and Susanna (silly women, as you would be ready to call them, if they were here now), these know more of the Messiah than all learned priests and rabbis; for it is the Spirit that searches all things, yes, the deep things of God...'[10]

---

[9] I am guessing that Priscilla, not Mary, is the 'I'..
[10] Quoted in Catie Gill and Elaine Hobby (2013) p25-26

George Fox, born in the 5th Month, 1624, in *Drayton* in *Leicestershire.* At 11 Years of Age knew Purity and Holiness; At the 19th Year of his Age in the year 1643 he left all, and travell'd up and down the Nation, visiting many People, who were seeking the Lord until the year 1646 that he enter'd into his more publick Ministrye.

For he was sent of God, as the Apostles were in the Primitive Times, to *turn people from Darkness to Light;* directing all to mind the Light of Christ Jesus in their own Hearts. So that in the year 1648 several Meetings of Friends were gather'd to God's Teaching, through his Ministry; in which Ministry he faithfully labour'd 44 Years through much Suffering and many Perils, of various sorts; as by his *Journal* of his Life doth largely appear.

And God gave him length of Days that he saw his Children, in the Faith, unto the Third and Fourth Generation, to a great Increase. And great was his Care for the Preservation of those who had received Truth, that they might walk in same; and to that end gave forth many faithful Epistles, and good Exhortations and Advice, for good Order and Discipline in the Church of Christ; as appears in the Collection of his *Epistles to Friends.*

He preached the Gospel effectually but two Days before he died, *viz.* on the 11th of the 11th Month, 1690 at *Gracious-Street* Meeting House After Meeting, he said, *I am glad I was here; now I am clear, I am fully clear;*

And then was the same Day taken ill of some Indisposition of Body, and continued weak in Body for two Days, at the House of *Henry Goldney,* in *White-Hart-Court* in

Gracious-Street; and lay in much Contentedness and Peace to the end, very sensible; in which time he mention'd divers Friends, and sent for some in particular, to whom he express'd his Mind for spreading Truth and Friends Books in the World; signifying also to some Friends, saying

> *All is well, and the Seed of God Reigns over all, and over Death itself; and that tho' I am weak in Body, yet the Power of the Lord is over all, and over all disorderly Spirit.*

Which were his wonted sensible Expressions, being in the Living Faith and Sense thereof, which he kept to the end.

And on the 13th of the 11th Month in 1690 he quietly departed this Life in Peace, about the 10th hour in the Night: So he ended his Days in a faithful Testimony, in perfect Love and Unity with his Brethren, being about the 66th Year of his Age.

Reflection

Private and public

Each of the four examples here combine the personal and the public in what they say and these, in turn, in, weave in and out of the editor's narrative. The one who has no other published words to her name, Elizabeth Braithwait, is here given most space for her spoken words These are quoted as being uttered at three separate moments in her last days.

In the first, Elizabeth and her mother are apparently alone together in some corner of her prison cell. Elizabeth, the dying daughter, is speaking almost as a teacher to her mother, in grief at their parting. "Here I am" she says, "content; and that is because I have made peace with God and can feel forgiveness to others; for God will be shortly setting me free from them". Her second saying is again spoken to a singular audience (to 'a Friend') but this time there is a stronger sense of a number of other intended listeners: those with whom, she says, she had often 'been Refreshed in our Meetings together'. What she says here is almost as an exhortation to Friends beyond to "keep your meetings, so that when it comes to your dying hour, you too will benefit from the strength they give you."

Lastly, Elizabeth addresses herself more intimately to her mother 'do not weep'), to her sister ('lie down by me') and finally, when words fail, to all those present ('taking her

Friends by the hand, with great Affection') – still wanting them to celebrate with her the comfort she now has gained from her vision of God's 'mercies and dealings'.

All this adds up to the words of a young woman dying in the horrible conditions of an overcrowded prison cell, incarcerated for the one cause that Friends today take for granted: the right to worship freely. Such is her passion for it that when words do finally fail – as they always must - she continues by 'singing in her heart' with a 'Cheerful countenance.'

On drafting

There is no clue in the account of Elizabeth's saying as to the presence of an editor. By contrast, in the origin and development of Stephen Crisp's written text, we are able to notice the part played by others. There are layers of attention, as it were, between speaker and listeners and between these listeners and their audience beyond. These layers of care seem to me to be extraordinarily touching. We get a sense of the Second Day Morning Meeting first hearing Stephen's short statement, and then asking other Friends to go away and gather more. We can imagine some of original witnesses later sitting round together, reminding each other of the things he had said in his last hours and then, having compiled them into a finished draft, bringing this back to the committee for acceptance – all in order to do justice to the person Stephen had been.

In presenting George Fox to us, the editor wants to stress the passionate life, with much already said by him in public, both written and spoken. There is then a subtle link to given to his last few spoken words, almost as if all that earlier body of work was a preparation: another kind of draft, for the most important words he had to offer us in the end.

On scribes

With these 'sayings', much of each text is presented as the spoken words of the author. For every speaker – uttering their saying in their dying moments - there would have been someone else taking some kind of notes, making a fair copy later: serving as a scribe (in a more positive sense than that referred to by Priscilla Cotton).

Among the trades in Ernest Taylor's list of the occupations of the early Friends who between 1652 and 1654 set off round the country as travelling minsters'[11] that of John Braithwaite[12] is given as 'shorthand writer'. It seems perfectly possible that others among early Friends may have had their own shorthand skills, including the editors of 'Piety Promoted' – which could certainly have been a help in recording the spoken words of a dying Friend.

Several times in the Sayings there would be an aside, suggesting that the scribe had difficulty reading their notes,

---

[11] Taylor ([1947] 1988) p41
[12] Whether he was related to Elizabeth, I don't know. I have copied for each the exact spelling used for the surname in each case.

let alone recalling all that the speaker had said. Elizabeth Moss for example was evidently a Friend who kept her scribe busy, speaking at length on several topics including recollections of her mother and exhortations to prayer by others. In the printed text, the narrative breaks off after some pages with this rather poignant note by the Friend at her bedside (my italics): 'This is the *Substance of but part of what she said, for she continued a considerable time*, speaking of the Mercies and Dealings of God to her Soul, and praising him for the same, to the Comfort of those present.' Other scribes evidently had other constraints, such as those that feature in the previous chapter for Mary Harris ('more sensible Expressions she uttered, which I omit for brevity') and Elizabeth Furley ('for brevity's sake omitted')

The relationship between the speaker and the writer – whether at the homely bedside or in a dank prison cell - must have been a partnership which varied – and those Friends who heard and recorded their words nearly always kept themselves anonymous. Very few of them named themselves. Just occasionally we can guess their identity, as we will find in Deborah Bell's account (in Chapter 5).

For a glimpse of George Fox's experience of scribal support for his published work, please take a look at Appendix 2. In that case we have the chance to know the scribe's identity. As to his dying saying, let alone any other of his writings, we just have to guess who scribed those with him.

3 SUFFERINGS

In compiling 'Piety Promoted', the editors wanted to promote piety, not celebrities. As they saw it, to understand the significance of their 'sayings', we need not just the words of these dying Friends but the context of the lives from which they had been spoken. Only then, the editors felt, could readers (or listeners) appreciate the divine grace which had led them. In John Tomkin's words,

> 'Some account I was obliged to give,
> concerning some of our dear Friends Sufferings and Labours in the Gospel, the better to let in the Reader to the understanding of the Weight, and indeed Meaning of some of their Expressions, not with purpose to exalt Men, but to Exalt the Great God, and his Grace in Christ Jesus, by which they were what they were." *(Introduction Vol. 1, part 1)*

As I discovered, the editors usually kept brief the detail of the persecutions and sufferings of the authors. For those picked out to reproduce in this collection, I have sought extra information from one or two other sources.

James Baines, who died in his early 50s (an old man in those days) is shown to have been a child with unusual gifts. From a young age he grew in eloquence. In his adult life, he combined the kindly encouragement to the newly convinced with stern words for any who became 'backsliders and unfaithful'. Despite the combination of 'distempers and infirmities' he suffered throughout his life, he inspired others with his 'sincerity and zeal' for the truth.

Two others - Henry Pontin and Jane Whitehead - give us a glimpse of the experiences endured at the hands of the justice system as a result of their public witness. Both opposed oath-swearing; both were punished for Quakers' insistence on the right to worship.

Edward Burrough, who also suffered long spells in prison and died there, spent all his life speaking out (and writing) for 'the truth' – and refusing (over and over again) to pay the tithes imposed by the established Anglican church.

Their words were published for their contemporaries – and for the others to come after them.

James Baines	1654-1505 (51)	Sedbergh
Henry Pontin	d. 1690s	Bristol
Jane Whitehead	d. 1674	Somerset
Edward Burrough	1635-1662 (27)	Cumbria[1]

---

[1] This is the modern name (since 1974) for Westmoreland - the name given in the original for Edward's birthplace and for that of many other early Friends.

James Baines, Son of *William* and *Sarah Baines,* of *Stangerthwait,* in the County of *Westmoreland,* was one who began to seek the Lord in his young Years; and as he grew in Sincerity and Zeal for the Blessed Truth, and increased in his Concern for the Promotion thereof; some time before he Died, God opened his Mouth in a publick Testimony, for the Lord Jesus Christ, and his pure Religion, in which he was very Fervent, having a sight (sic) how eminently God would appear for those who were Faithful; and he had a *word of Encouragement to them; but sharp in Judgement to the Backsliders[2] and Unfaithful:*

And altho' he was under much Affliction, by reason of Bodily Infirmities and Distempers which grew upon him; yet he was more and more devoted to Truths Service (as if he had known that his time was not to be long in this World) even to within some Hours that his last Sickness seized upon him.

And notwithstanding he was under great Pain and Exercise of Body, yet the Power and Presence of the Lord was with him, which was his great Support and Strength; and he often spake of the goodness of God to his Soul, and of that inward Sweetness, Peace and Comfort, that the Lord was pleased to

---

[2] *Backsliding'* was a term used to mean 'failure to attend Meeting for Worship sufficiently frequently.' To appreciate its significance, we need to remember this was a time when the Society had yet to establish formal membership, and behaviour in line with 'Gospel order' an essential to Quaker Identity (Roads 2019 p15).

afford unto him in his green afflictions to the great Satisfaction of those who were present.

He gave much wholesome Advice in the time of his Sickness to Friends and others, and spake of the Prosperity of Truth, and said in particular to his Relations, as followeth:

As we are Children of believing Parents and hath had our Education amongst Friends, so I would not have you to rest Contented there, but be Solid, and Weighty, and Humble your selves under the mighty hand of God, and as you abide there, you will feel the goodness of the Lord to spring in your Souls, to your great Comfort, and inward Peace and Satisfaction.

I know our Natural Tempers are inclinable to be Light and Airy, like other People, therefore we have more occasion to be bowed and weighty in our Minds;

and speaking concerning Tythes, *he desired Friends would keep up their Testimony against them,* for said he, *I could have slipt* (sic) *Sufferings, if I would have given way to it, but it was a thing I durst not do, but I accounted it a great Mercy that the Lord had Blessed me with something to part with for his Name and Truth sake* And altho' he suffered pretty much at times, upon the account of Tythes, yet the Lords goodness to him, did over-balance all, so that he had *a word of Incouragement to others on that Account.*

Upon occasion, speaking of the uncertainty of Riches, he said, at some time, *I persued them, and they fled from me*, but this use he said he made of it; to conclude, *it is not a City here I was to seek after, but one in the Heavens, whose maker and builder is God*, this he spake *as Caution to others*.

And at several times he expressed *his great Peace with God here, and full Assurance of Eternal Blessedness in the World to come, thro' the Atonement made by the Lord Jesus Christ, and the Work of Sanctification of his Spirit*; the Day before he died, hearing that the Antient Friend *Ann Camm* was deceased, he said, *Ah! That honest Honourable Woman, is she gone to her Eternal Rest before me? I shall follow her very shortly, where we shall meet never to part again.*

Many were the comfortable Expressions and seasonable Advice which he gave forth in his Sickness, that cannot be Remembered, and as in his Life time he honoured the Truth, so was his latter end Comfortable, and full of Peace.

In which, he departed this Life, the first of the tenth Month, 1705 Aged 51 Years – and was Buried at Friends Burying-Ground, at *Sedbergh* Meeting House

....

Postscript: the Testimony of *Isaac Alexander,* concerning *James Baines*, in a Letter dated the eighth of the tenth Month 1705, who also Died the 11th of the 12th Month after him:

"Our truly Beloved and Esteemed Friend *James Baines* departed this Life the first of this Instant; and tho' he was afflicted with great Pain, yet he bore it with admirable Patience, for tho' I live remote from him, and notwithstanding my unfitness, I went often to visit him, and I don't remember that since I came amongst Friends, any Friend so Universally visited by all sorts of People as he was, especially by faithful Friends; neither did I ever visit a Friend in such a Case, who had that Reach upon all sorts of People, both In the Expressions that he declared in the time of his Sickness; and also the Frame of his Spirit, it was admirable Reaching and Melting, beyond what I can express; and so continued to the End, as Sweet and sensible as Ever.

He Died with the greatest Esteem and Love to Friends and Truth, and in great Esteem and Interest in the Hearts of Friends; he Died in a most Happy and Blessed Condition."

Isaac Alexander

Henry Pontyn[3] of *French-Hay* Meeting, was a Faithful Labourer in the Ministry of our Lord Jesus Christ, as well beyond Sea, as in this Nation of *England,* and endured many Sufferings and Hardships, and several Years Imprisonments at *Gloucester,* for his Faithful Testimony for God, and continued Faithful to his Death –

on his dying Bed he said, *that the Lord had done well for me, and the Chastizements of the Lord are good; Exhorting his Children and Friends about him, to Live in the Fear of the Lord, that they might Die in his Favour;* saying, *the End will Crown all.*

He died in the sixty seventh Year of his Age.

....

Historical note

This is the briefest of the 'Sayings' that I found.
From another source, it is clear that the sufferings that Henry and others endured for their 'crimes' were indeed many. Joseph Besse, the author of the considerable record of 17th century Quaker sufferings[4] gives this fuller idea of their persecutors and of the punishments and abuse they inflicted:

---

[3] Spelled Pontin in the Besse text (next page) and subsequent sources
[4] Besse (1753) p218-222

"*Anno 1677* In this Year *John Meredith*, a Justice of the Peace, signalized (sic) himself by fiercely prosecuting the *Quakers*: He caused 27 of them to be indicted at *Glocester* Sessions, for Absence from the National Worship, though he knew that most of them had deeply suffered before by the Act against Conventicles: He arbitrarily required of **Henry Pontin** and *Nathanial Hopkins* Sureties for their good Behaviour, when no Complaint was made against them, and kept them in Prison three Months, after which he indicted them at the Sessions for Meetings, and had them fined 40*l.* each, and continued in Prison: He beat William Benet and William Wade unmercifully with his own Hands; and took John Selcock by the Hair of the Head, and pluckt him out of the Meeting-house at *French-hay*, into the Yard., then drew his Knife and said he would mark him, but was prevented by the interposition of his Clerk and others...

Anno 1681 The Justices at their Sessions in the Month called *January* this year ....tendred them the Oath of Allegiance, and sent them to Prison for refusing it. And for the same Cause, (24 names, of whom 13 women) were committed to Prison: Some of the Women had Children sucking at their Breasts, and others of them were with Child, and the Prison being out of Repair, they were much incommoded for want of Room. The Men were afterward indicted at Sessions, for refusing the Oath, and brought in *Guilty*, and were said to be *Premunired*, though Sentence was not publickly read: both Men and Women were recommended to Prison. Soon after this **Henry Pontin**, *Henry Ashby* and *Ralph Langley*, were also sent to Gaol for refusing to swear."

Jane Whitehead, wife of Tho. *Whitehead,* of *North-Cadbury* in *Somerset;* her Maiden Name was *Jane Vaugh,* born in *Westmoreland,* her Relations living about *Hutton* in the same County, whom she left in Obedience to the Lord, and travelled in his Service; and did bear Witness against the false Ways and Worships of the World, and for the sake of her Testimony endured much Persecution.

And in the Year 1655, coming to *Banbury in Oxfordshire,* to visit her dear Friend, *Ann Audland,* then a Prisoner for the Truth; and she for bearing Witness for the Truth, and against their Cruelty and Wickedness, was taken and committed to Prison, and lay there five Weeks; and not long after, coming again to the said Town the Magistrates tendred (sic) her the Oath of Abjuration; which she refusing for Christ's sake, who said, *Swear not at all,* she was imprisoned 12 months in a low wet nasty Place, in the Winter Season, that sometimes she would be over Shoes in Water; and she did endure this in much Patience.

In the 4th month 1662, she was again Imprisoned at the said *Banbury* for the Worshipping of God, at a Meeting of the People called Quakers, where she lay in the same nasty Prison three Months. These things she suffered before she was Married. Afterwards *Thomas Whitehead,* abovesaid (sic) took her to be his Wife, by whom she had five Children that she left behind her.

And again, at *Ivelchester* she endured five Months Imprisonment, with a young Child Sucking at her Breast, in a cold Winter, for speaking the words of Truth and Soberness to the Priest of *North-Cadbury*; but the Lord did uphold her by the Word of his Power, in the manifold Exercises and Tribulations which she passed through, too tedious here to relate. – Those Abuses which she endured, brought her tender body into weakness, which did attend her several Years before she Died; and under the great Exercises and Weakness of Body, she acknowledged, *That the Lord was wonderful good to Her.*

And did often say, *That the Lord had broken in upon her, and with his heavenly Presence, did fill her, to the Comfort of her Soul.* And said, *O that the Lord may never take his Presence from me.* And to the last was kept sensible, and declared, *That she had the Testimony of God's Love, and that it would be well with her; and that she had no desire to live any longer in this World.* And *Charged her Children to be Obedient to their Father; and that they should mind Truth, and then the Blessing of the Lord would be with them.*

And the Morning before she died, being sensible her Death was at hand, told a Friend, *that she has going to her long home.* And soon after departed this Life, in the Love and Peace of God, on the 28th Day of the 7th Month, 1674.

Edward Burroughs[5], born in *Westmoreland* about the year 1635, of honest Parents; he was in his childhood ripe of Knowledge, and did far excel his Years; and grey Hairs was upon him, when but a Youth; inclinable to the best Things, and the nearest way of Worship to the Scriptures, accompanying the best Men...

And when it pleased God to visit his People in the North of *England*, This Servant of Christ was early called, *viz* Anno.1652, when about seventeen Years of Age; and was sent forth by the Spirit of the Lord to preach the Everlasting Gospel...and was an able Minister of the Glad-Tidings of Salvation, in most parts of *England* and through *Ireland* several times, and in *Scotland* and *Flanders* his ministry was made effectual by the mighty Power of God, in turning many Thousands from Darkness to Light....His industry in the Lord's Work was very great, had seldom many Hours Repose, making the Lord's Work his whole Business, not taking so much Liberty as to spend one Week to himself, about any outward Occasion, in ten Years....

At the age of 19, *Anno* 1654, he came up to *London*, was one of the first that preached in that City; and great Opposition he met there, but God made his Ministry effectual, to the Conversion of Hundreds; he continued about *London* very much, at times, between 8 or 9 Years, speaking of the Things of the Kingdom of God: His Heart was much drawn towards

---

[5] Spelled Burrough in all subsequent sources

London, and he did often say, when Sufferings came for Gospel's sake, - *I can freely go to that City* (i.e. London) *and Lay down my Life for a Testimony of that Truth which I have declared thro' the Power and Spirit of God.*

And in the Year 1662, visiting Friends in the City of *Bristol*, he took his leave, and said to very many - *I am going up to the City of London, and Suffer among Friends in that place.*

And a little after his return to that City, was taken from a Meeting of the People of God, call'd Quakers, at *Bull and Mouth*, by Soldiers, under the Command of *Sr. Richard Brown*, Mayor, and committed to *Newgate* by the said Mayor, not for Evil-doing, but for Testifying to the Name of the Lord Jesus, and for the Worship of God, and there lay in Prison, with six or seven Score Friends more, upon the same Account, many being shut up among Felons, in nasty Places; and for want of Prison-room, grew weak, sickned and dyed, among which this young Man was one; his Sickness increasing upon him daily, tho' in much Patience he was carried thro' all; in Prayer often both Day and Night, saying at one time, *I have had a Testimony of the Lord's Love to me from my Youth, and my Heart hath been given up to do his Will; I have preached the Gospel freely in this City, and have often given up my Life for the Gospel's sake: Lord rip open my Heart, and see if it be not right before thee.*

Another time he said, *There lies no Iniquity at my door; but the Presence of the Lord is with me, and his Life I feel*

Justifies me. Afterwards he said to the Lord, *Thou hast loved me when I was in the Womb, and I have loved thee from my Cradle, and from my Youth unto this day; and have served thee Faithfully in my Generation,* And he spake to Friends that were about him, *to live in love and Peace, and love one another:* And said *The Lord take the Righteous from the Evil to come:* And prayed for his Enemies and Persecutors, and said, *Lord forgive* Richard Brown *who imprisoned me.*

Again he said, *That tho this Body of Clay must return to Dust, yet, I have this Testimony that I have served God in my Generation, and that Spirit which hath lived and acted, and ruled in me, shall yet break forth in Thousands.*

And in the Morning before he departed, being sensible of his Death, said, *Now my Soul and Spirit is centred in its own Being, with God, and this form of Person, may return from whence it was taken.* And after a little season gave up the Ghost, as a Martyr for the Word of God, and Testimony of Jesus.

Reflection

In seventeenth century England the general context, to put it bluntly, was that 'death lived nearby and might visit at any time'[6]. Children died young. Witnessing a loved one dying painfully through hunger, ill-health, long-drawn-out disease, let alone persecution and wretched conditions in prison would have been an experience that was all too common. And this is to say nothing of the agonies of childbirth, with families of living children having to endure stillbirths and infant mortality in between.

In the present day, there is certainly much inequality and routine violence in the world, as well as the hostility and destitution faced by migrants taking long and dangerous journeys in search of sanctuary. But in Britain we can only imagine two other things faced by our forebears. First, a world in which warfare was so close to home The first English Civil War (1642-46) may be the only one that many of us recall from school history lessons: but the 'wars of the three kingdoms' lasted fourteen years. Second, there was the web of legislation to catch and punish dissent – and in particular, to quell Quaker meetings.

---

[6] Spufford (1981) p201

48

New laws criminalised Quakers for persisting in their own way of worship. The Quaker Act of 1662 and the Conventicle Act of 1664 (applied to all Dissenters) made it illegal for more than four persons to meet for worship otherwise than in the practice of the Anglican Church. Punishment meant suffering for whole families, as well as for individuals.

Tithe-paying

In addition, a major issue for early Friends was their outrage at the compulsory tax charged at the time for the upkeep of Anglican clergy and buildings. Along with other nonconformists, for them the tithe-paying system had long been objectionable. They saw it as 'anti-Christian' and its enforcement, an oppression. A refusal to pay these tithes was an extremely risky stance to take 'which cost many dearly in terms of loss of property or incarceration[7] - but Quakers 'made it an 'article of Faith' [8]

As early as 1653, to coincide with one of his preaching journeys in an area where a tithe strike was beginning. George Fox had published a passionate tract on the subject. Rosemary Moore helps us hear him with this extract:

> 'There are such priests as take Tythes... they that
> will not give them they sue at the law. Beside   the
> Tithe-corn [they] take ten shillings for preaching

---

[7] Rogers Healey (2013) p60
[8] Dale Spencer, (2013) p142

Funeral Sermons.... And Easter Reckonings and Midsummer dues and money for churching of women, and thus by every device get money and burthen poor people that labour very hard and can scarce get food and raiment'.[9]

Refusal to pay tithes was a constant feature of early Quaker witness: a cause against which they testified, heart and soul. As a result, fines were imposed, and refusal to pay them meant imprisonment and their homes and possessions being ruthlessly 'despoiled.'

Nonviolent protest

The constant nonviolent protest by early Quakers against such outrages lit a fire that has persisted in various forms in the life of the Religious Society of Friends ever since.

'As a Palestinian Quaker woman, I have confronted structures of injustice all my life' writes Jean Zaru[10].

> '"Normal life" for Palestinians living in the Occupied Territories has disappeared. The apartheid wall continues to be built on confiscated land, separating people from their lands, families, schools, hospitals, and houses of worship... Palestinians are traumatized by the daily violence of an armed military occupation, which affects both their physical and mental

---

[9] Moore (2013) p17
[10] Zaru (2008) p56 and 61

health.....Violence, after all, is not only about war and weaponry....We must continue to fan the embers of light no matter how small they are, because these embers of light give hope to those in the forefront of the struggle'.

It was just for a short time that I myself stayed in Palestine in 2009 as one of an international (and multidenominational) team of peace volunteers[11] - and while there was able, briefly, to meet Jean. Years later I met her at a Quaker event in Brussels. Both journeys, in my case, were relatively straightforward. But hers were not. Like the founding Friends, she - as a member of the World Council of Churches, and other bodies - has had to travel in her ministry: in her case to attend meetings across Europe and in the United States. To leave her own country she has had to find expensive fees. Each time, she has had to have checked, military permits, papers, identity cards, passports and her body. In terms of travel expenses, the price of the journey (in her words) is as nothing compared to 'the pain, the humiliation, the fatigue and the anxiety.'[12]

For those unable to meet her in person, Jean's gift is her written accounts from firsthand experience. In the same way, today's Quaker peacebuilders in Africa - whom we in Britain

---

[11] Ecumenical Accompaniment Programme for Peace in Palestine and Israel https://www.quaker.org.uk/our-work/international-work/eappi
[12] Zaru (2008) p10-11

have little chance of physically meeting - reach us on the published page. Hezron Masitsa, for example, writes:

> 'I was born into a Quaker family and raised with grandparents who were among the first Quaker converts in western Kenya.'

After some years working as warden in a Quaker centre in Nairobi Kenya, he still continues with peacebuilding work today, explaining:

> 'The experiences of my mother and other family members increased my motivation for peace and encouraged me to see peacebuilding as a lifestyle and not a project that is undertaken just when there is conflict in a nation.   National conflicts are a reflection of conflicts at family level...especially in the treatment of women.' [13]

As Hezron wrote elsewhere, 'The 2007-2008 post-election violence was such a challenge to Kenyan Quakers'[14]

Driven by the same commitment to answer that of God within others as impelled those in seventeenth century England, the descendants of those founding Friends continue their ministry across continents. From the sufferings they too endure, the same passion – also captured in their own words - renews them and the rest of us.

---

[13] Mombo (2016) p47-49
[14] Chico (2014) p67

4 CONNECTIONS

What is the impact on us now of reading these texts from the past? For me, they remind me of roots I barely knew I had. The excitement remains in imagining how early Friends might have listened to them being read aloud together. But I have also come to appreciate the opposite: namely, the comfort and strength to be had in silent, solitary reading.

'Piety'

After a series of attempts to find definitions and theological meanings of this word (the first in the collection's title), I remembered to try and practise what we Quakers still preach: search for the various messages the word might give and listen for the spirit within.

Until now, I had assumed both piety and pious people to be dutiful, scriptural and solemn matters. In these accounts of early Quakers, however, I found three qualities emerging that suggested the kind of piety that the editors wanted to promote. These qualities came across as: **passion, commitment** and **humility**. From examples in this chapter I hope to show how these, in different ways, seem to shine out in each individual.

First, William Stovey: both a 'zealous encourager' of others in the protest against the tithe system; a 'great sufferer'; and one who showed forgiveness towards his persecutors.

From a more domestic context, Mary Padley's piety shines from her everyday behaviour ('conversation'), her charity to the poor – and her commitment to God, throughout the agonies of childbirth.

Far from being a quietly pious figure, William Gibson left his soldier life to set out as a preacher who was both 'terrible' in his fury at hypocrisy and 'tender' towards the vulnerable.

Elizabeth Barker's piety has been arrived at through a long period of convincement and in her last hours, having come to terms with her God and her end.

A humble figure, John Carlisle 'sometimes opened to speak a few Words... sometimes to supplicate the Lord, and other times in Silence': a committed teacher.

William Stovey	d 1705		
Mary Padley	1663-1695	(29)	London
William Gibson	1629-1684	(55)	Lancaster
Elizabeth Barker	1673-1701	(28)	London
John Carlisle	1632-1707	(75)	Carlisle

William Stovey received Truth (as it is professed by the People called Quakers) upon its first Publication in those Parts and was a very Zealous Encourager of Faithfulness among Friends.

He also receiv'd a Gift of the Ministry, and was often very much concerned in his Travels, that Truth's Testimony might be kept up in its several Branches, and particularly against the Antichristian Oppression of *Tythes*, &c. For bearing which Testimony, as well as keeping up of Meetings, he was a great Sufferer; being cast into several Prisons, and had his Cattle, and other Goods, several times taken from him, even to the Bed he lay on, and almost all that was thought worth removing.

His last Sickness was not very great in appearance, nor long, yet he signified he should never go forth of his Chamber, and said, *I can and do forgive all my Enemies.* He was very cheerful in the time of his Illness, and more than ordinary glad of Friends Company, that came to see him, and said, he was *satisfied and willing, when the Lord pleased, to leave this World, in Expectation of a far greater Happiness in that which is to come.*

Mary Padley, Wife of *John Padley*, Timber-Merchant, of *Olaves, Southwark*, a Woman adorn'd with Truth and Innocency, Chaste, Upright, and Sincere Hearted; Industrious, yet void of Covetousness; so that Vertue did shine forth in her Conversation:

She was also Charitable to the Poor, Plain in Apparel, Adorning the Truth in her Conversation, punctual in performing her Promise, and in the discharge of any Trust reposed in her.

And as she spent her Days in the Fear of God, so the Lord was Gracious to her at her Death: She was taken with Pains of Travail, in Childbearing, the 6th of the 7th Month, 1695 at which time she said, in much tenderness and fervency of Spirit, *My God and my Father, Deliver me:* And after she was delivered, *She praised God for his Mercies towards her:*

And after, being asked by her Husband, how she did? (finding some unusual Symptoms attend her) she answered, *Weak, but well satisfied:* And as a Confirmation thereof, broke forth into *sweet Praises to the Lord.* And died, leaving behind her 4 Young Children, Aged about 28 Years.

William Gibson, born In Caton nr Lancaster about 1629, being a Soldier in the Garrison in Carlisle Cumberland; and he with three others, understanding that a Preacher called a *Quaker*, who was a Stranger, had appointed a Meeting in that City, agreed to go together to the Meeting, with an intent to abuse the said Friend, whose Name was Thomas Holmes; William coming first to the Meeting, and hearing the Friend powerfully declaring the Truth, was so affected and reached by his Testimony, that he stept up into the Meeting, near the place where Thomas Holmes stood, knowing the designs of his Fellows, waited to defend the Friend, and bid any that durst offer to abuse him;

from which time he became a constant frequenter of Friends meetings, and quitted his Place in the Garrison, and employ'd himself in the Trade of Shoomaking,... married Eliz Thompson, settled in Sankey Meeting near Warrington for some years, and some were convinced of Truth by his ministry, who continue Faithful to this Day, and many others confirmed to the Blessed Truth, so that his memorial is of good Savour in those Parts. He afterwards travelled Southwards in Work of the Gospel, was imprisoned at Maidestone in Kent for his Testimony, which Imprisonment was long; from whence being discharged, went to *London* and

removed his Wife and Family thither, where his Service was well known to Friends in that City, and many other Parts of the Nation, and many are the seals of his Minister;

and tho' he was severe in Reproof, and terrible in his Ministry to the Hypocrite, and the Workers of Iniquity, yet he was as a tender Father to the Mourners in Zion (sic)....a lover of Unity among Brethren...devoted to the Service of God... an example to Believers... suffer'd hard Imprisonments and the spoiling of his Goods, for his Testimony sake.

In the third month, 1684, he travelled to his native country, Lancaster... taken sick of Ague and Feaver at Coventry, and got to London...

On his sick bed, he exhorted others who came to visit him to *Faithfulness, and Trust and Confidence in the Lord....* He left two Sons and one Daughter, to whom he gave Good Advice.... And he charged them to

> *avoid all vain and idle Company, and to be diligent in frequenting the Assemblies of the Lords People, and to have an Ear open to receive the good council and advice of them who fear the Lord...*

Thus did this good Man like Abraham, charge his Children to walk before the Lord; he was very resigned, and given up to Die, and expressed his Love to the Brethren; saying,

> *my Love in the Lord Jesus is to all Faithful; and Remember my Dear Love unto them, and to all the Faithful Labourers....*

Elizabeth Barker late Wife of *John Barker*, Merchant in *Tower-Street, London*, being Sick, a Friend went to visit her; when she understood that he was below, she caused those present to withdraw, and sent for him up; who asking, 'how she did?' She Wept, and said,

> *I am a poor weak Woman; and I have prayed to the Lord, that if I am to dye of this Sickness, he would let me know it; and I do not see it yet, tho' I am weak enough to expect it.*

And she expressed *much concern for her three Children, if she should be taken away.* The Friend answered, It was true, that Children are very near to tender Parents, but we ought to be resign'd, and commit them to God, who gave them to us.... Upon which she seem'd somewhat satisfied, and after a space of silence, she said,

> *It is Assurance of my Peace with God, that I do earnestly desire.* And further said, *For these two Years past, God has been at work in my Heart, and I have endeavoured to answer his Will, and have deny'd my self of some things, but I have had a care not to do it in the Imitation of others, but from a Conviction in my own Conscience; and I hope, if I live, I shall be Faithful to God,*

and said moreover, *And to keep those Convenants that I have made with God.* And after some space, she said,

> *Oh the Presence of God! It is that which my soul desires to enjoy; - God has been good to me many times; for when I have been alone at home, as well*

as at Meetings, the Lord has broken in upon my Heart; and when I have been troubled, and exercised in my Mind, I have gone in secret, and prayed to the Lord, and I know he has heard me, and several times answered my Prayer, not only for my self, but for my Children also.

About three days before her last, she tells the visitor:
that *she was willing to dye, if it was the Will of God.*
[Being at peace with God, as she felt it, was the outcome of penitence, through an inner struggle]:

I have loved vain and foolish Things; but I have prayed to the Lord to forgive me all my Sins: and now, instead of that fear of Death, there is much Sweetness upon my Soul; and all those vain things I have loved, I now loath; and all the World is nothing to me...

[She then grew weaker] and *gave Directions concerning the ordering of her Children and Family, and also where she would be buried*; and she did receive *Assurance of her future Happiness....*

The Voice said, submit, submit; and I say, I have submitted, I have submitted;

or to the same effect. When these Words were spoken, a Relation present said, Thou art going to leave us; she reply'd *I shall be happy.*

John Carlisle [born, Carlisle; 'by trade a Tanner']

.... Grew and increased in Faithfulness, according to his Measure: And was drawn forth sometimes in a Publick Testimony, and preached the Gospel, not in the Eloquence of Speech, but very Powerful and Reaching, and in Simplicity, and Sincerity; altho' illiterate as to outward Learning; yet in his Doctrine, and Testimony, considerably opened the Scriptures of Truth, by the Assistance of that Holy Spirit that gave them forth, to the Edification of the Hearers, and Confirmation of those Gospel Truths by him preached.

He laboured in the Work of the Ministry, in divers Counties... and several were convinced by his Labours of Love, in the Gospel of Christ in many Places, and remain as Seal of his Ministry. He was open-hearted and zealous for the Testimony of Truth, and in much Love received the Friends of it, that travelled in the same Work, into his House.

And as he delighted to draw near to the Well-spring of Life, for Divine Succour and Consolation; he was not unmindful often to wait upon the Lord in his Family, unto who the Lord was pleased to reach, in order to their Convincement by his blessed Truth and was sometimes opened to speak a few Words unto them of Information, or Exhortation, and sometimes to supplicate the Lord; and other times in

Silence, to wait upon the Lord in his Family, to feel an Encrease and Growth in the Vertue of Truth among them.

And many are Witnesses of the Benefit and Comfort they received in those his Family-Meetings, that have been at them: So that although at his first Convincement in the City, and when he came to bear Testimony to the Truth, he was as a speckled Bird[1], among the Birds of the Wood, there being none that bore the same Profession in the said City, and was warred against by the bitter Magistrates, and severe Informers, and cruel Prosecutors...

He was always ready to help forward, and Encourage every good Work on Truths Account, and was much given to Hospitality, and open hearted to the Poor of any Society. He was of a blameless Conversation, just in his Dealings, and of a good Report among all People, and Valiant for Truth and its Testimony unto the End. And in his Sickness often exhorted Friends to be Faithful to the Lord and his Truth, according to their Measure, saying

> *Then the Lord should stand by them, and bring them through all the Exercises they might meet with for the same, and they should have the Reward of well done;*

---

[1] For this a likely source seems to be the *Book of Jeremiah* 12:9, "Mine heritage is unto me as a speckled bird, the birds round about are against her; come ye, assemble all the beasts of the field, come to devour."

with more Expressions of the like Nature.

And having some sight of the Glory and Joys of Heaven...he signified his desire of a Change, and that his Wife and Children might give him freely up, saying, *It would be well,* and being sensible, the time of his Departure drew near, said to his Friends and Neighbours present, that *a little time would finish and make all things Easie.*

And in about half an Hour passed away, being the 25th of the Month 1706, and died in the Faith of Jesus, and in full Unity with Friends, having born an innocent Testimony for Truth in his Generation, and left a good Savour behind him. Aged about 74 years.

Reflection

Every time I read John Carlisle, I feel a surge of tenderness for the man and his (less visible) editor. Passion, commitment and humility: both of them seem good exemplars of all three. And so too, in their different ways, the other three Friends: channels for the spirit, living the essential effort of Quaker worship: to listen, to wait and to minister, as 'Publishers of Truth', right up to their last breath.

The commitment of early Friends to set up a sustainable organisation is widely recognised. I feel moved also to learn that its basis was not one of rules, first and foremost, but rather of spiritual fellowship, to 'bear with one with another, to be helpful one unto one another, and in true and tender love to watch over another'[2].

Silent waiting

The power of this sense of 'a company met together... in unity of spirit' gave rise to Edward Burrough's recollection that

> '... waiting upon the Lord in silence as often we did for many hours together, with our minds and hearts towards Him.... we received often the pouring down of the Spirit upon us...

---

[2] Brayshaw ([1921] 1982) p114

and our hearts were made glad, and our tongues
loosed, and our mouths opened.' [3]

Silent waiting is not often mentioned in the deathbed
scenes of the Piety Promoted collection, but that may be
because it was too obvious an activity for contemporary
Friends to need mentioning - as suggested in Thomas
Upsher's reference (in the next chapter) to the

> great Refreshment felt many times in being with
> him in Silence, in time of his Sickness.

For our present time, as Diana Lampen reminds us, this
refreshment remains a powerful gift:

> 'Quakers do have something very special to offer
> the dying and the bereaved, namely that we are
> at home in silence. Not only are we thoroughly
> used to it and unembarrassed by it, but we know
> something about sharing it, encouraging others in
> its depths and above all, letting ourselves be used
> to it.' [4]

During the months of working on these sayings , I have
periodically fallen into dark times of gloom and lost the
original joy of discovery. Voices in my head complained:
these are boring to read! No-one else will be interested!
And then I found that what led me back to the joy was
something quite simple. Picking up the physical volume
from the table - usually early morning or late at night -

---

[3] Op cit p 119
[4] Lampen (1978) p22

holding the weight of it in my hand, checking a name in the index, turning to the page and becoming immersed again – in silence. No reading aloud. Just following in silence the lines of print on those small, worn-out pages and listening to the voices of those who had made their own discovery – and given their lives to it.

Then and now

Today's Quaker world is very different from that of Mary Padley, William Gibson, or the others. On the one hand, the movement they joined was growing from a few hundred to forty thousand, through the insights of a few pioneers in a corner of north west England. Today's Quakers, on the other, belong to a global population of over 400,000 Friends, spread out in four sections:

- Europe and Middle East
- the Americas
- Asia/West Pacific and
- Africa

and grouped in four overall 'flavours' as to their ways of worship. Many present-day Quakers, let alone anyone else, may be unaware that world gatherings take place every few years. It may also be news to others (as it has been to me) to learn that in recent years the first Sunday of October every year has become World Quaker Day: a chance to appreciate the family of Quakers in worship at the same time. As the Friends World Committee for Consultation puts it, 'the Quaker community circles the globe, spanning a rich diversity of regional cultures, beliefs and styles of worship.'. [5]

It is also a community which still connects with Elizabeth Barker's simple hope: 'Oh the presence of God! It is that which my soul desires to enjoy'.

---

[5] Friends World Committee for Consultation
http://fwcc.world/about-fwcc

5 PARTINGS

When does our dying begin? For some, it seems death had been a long time coming. In these sayings, the one facing death is not by any means the only one with something to say. Others present want to question them, not least to check if they are 'alright' or to persuade them not to go. The editors want to introduce them to us, their later readers.

In this chapter, four Friends take their leave. From the portrait of Richard Vokins as a kindly employer and father, there has to be extra sympathy for his wife: not only for her imminent bereavement, but also at her having to accept, after his death, the prospect of their empty apple orchard as 'punishment' for his stand against tithes.

The account of Deborah Bell was published in the seventh volume of dying sayings, edited by her husband John[1]. He leaves it a while to enable readers to realise that link – and to recognise his identity in the affecting exchange between them as they finally part company. She died in 1738. The seventh volume was published just two years later, his grief still raw. He is present in three timescales: as scribe at his wife's deathbed, as editor at his desk and as our companion in reading his posthumous script of her spoken words.

---

[1] See Appendix 3

Alexander Jaffray grew up among Presbyterians in Aberdeen. His is a message to a larger audience than nearby family or Friends; and his death did not come until he had completed the work God had for him to do - with the striking metaphor of the 'stink' of a candle going out contrasted with the 'savour' left by his own ending.

Thomas Upsher, the last in this group of farewells, had evidently been facing his death over some time. The description of spiritual growth through his life tells of his early 'waiting upon the Lord in silence', to gaining the 'gift to speak', becoming an 'able Minister' and serving the cause. Just before his death, he ministers at another's grave for an hour and a half. Then in his final hours, he returns to silence - finding comfort at last, together with those around him.

Richard Vokins   d 1696   West Charlow, Herts
Deborah Bell   1689-1738 (49) Bradford, London
Alexander Jaffray   1624-1673 (49) Aberdeen
Thomas Upsher   1672-1704 (32) Colchester

Richard Vokins,

brother to the aforesaid *Thomas Vokins* [son of *Richard* and *Joan Vokins* of West *Charlow* in the County of *Berks*].

In the time of his Sickness, he kept feeding in Retirement within, and when he first took his Bed, he examin'd himself before the Lord thus; saying,

> *Lord, have I done any thing to offend thee, have I wronged any Man?*

And desiring the Lord would take off all Reproach from off his People; and during his Sickness, he was preserved in a Quiet Frame of Mind, no impatient Words coming from him; expressing how the Lord had *preserved him in true Simplicity, which was his great Comfort, and gave good Advice to several who came to see him;* saying to them

> *It is well with me, you cannot think what I enjoy.*

In the time of his Health, he was an Humble, tender-hearted Man, Considerate of his Servants, and Poor People that Worked for him; often saying, *that he would not Inrich himself out of their Labours.* And was glad when he could do good to any; one time he called for his two Children and *prayed the Lord to bless them; his Wife asked him if it did not seem hard to part with them, to which he replied, no, all is well*; desiring his Dear Children might take him *for an Example, and live no worse a Life than he had done.*

After this, his Wife said, the Lord is able to raise thee again if it bee his Will; he replied,

> *I know he is able, but he doth not intend to restore*
> *me again;*

And he told his Doctor *he could do him no Good;* in the time of his Sickness, the Impropriator (sic) and Servants cleared his Orchard of Apples to the Value of four Pound for Tythes; his Wife asked if those People Plundering them, did not trouble him, he replied,

> *no, not at all, the Lord forgive them, they know not*
> *what they do.*

When his Wife perceived his Speech to alter; she again asked him, *if he was willing to leave the World?* He replied, *yes, very willing.*

Soon after his Speech went quite away, and next Day he died in Peace; being the twelfth of the eighth Month, 1696.

Deborah Bell [2]

[daughter of John and Deborah Wynn, active early Friends; started preaching at age 19; suffered from pleurisy in her last months, but went on in ministry until the last weeks of her life]

Being under a concern to visit a few more meetings she traveled to Hertfordshire, and though in a weak state of health, she undertook that journey, which proved her last, towards the middle of the 7th month 1738. She was from home ten days and had six meetings and yet although weak in body, yet she appeared strong in her ministry.

The last time she was at the evening meeting at Bromley, about two weeks before she died, she bore a living testimony to the truth, and was concerned in supplication to the Lord in a particular manner; and in great fervency, prayed for the preservation, growth, and settlement of the young amongst us, in the living eternal truth, to the affecting and tendering of many ears.

When she came home from the meeting, she was filled with divine comfort, and said

---

[2] This saying, as you will notice, has none of the extra capital letters of the others. I copied it in the last hour of a day in February 2020 at Friends House library where the volume is kept and not to be borrowed. The travel restrictions of the pandemic since then has prevented me returning to insert these As a rare example of scribe and author relationship, this felt too important a treasure to leave it out. See appendix 3 for the full reference.

*'it is now finished, I do not expect you will have me
with you at that meeting any more...*

When her pain was very great, she expressed herself at times
after the following manner;

*This is hard work indeed, one had need to have
nothing else to do at such a time as this; I am sure it
is as much as I am able to endure, to bear the
afflictions of the body; one had not need to have
terror of mind besides.*

And appealing to the young woman standing by her, whom
she dearly loved, and who had duly attended to her in her
illness, said,

*Thou knowest I have had very little respite from
pain since I was first taken ill; I would have none put
off that great work of repentance until such a time as
this; if I had that work to do, what a dreadful thing it
would be!*

At a time when divers young people were present, she said,

*I would have our young people be willing to bear the
cross in their youth, and despise the same, for that is
the way to have true peace in themselves.* And
another time she said, *I now feel that which my soul
has longed for.....*

Observing the distress I was in, she looked earnestly upon
me, and said,

the Lord brought us together and has been with us and thou must give me freely up to Him again, and he will support thee, and take care of thee.

Again, being in deep distress of mind, under the consideration of my great loss of so dear a companion, if she should be removed, I asked her if she had not rather live with me a little longer, if Providence saw meet; she looked pleasantly upon me, and after a little pause said,

I have no desire nor will of my own; I stand in the will of God....

I told her if Providence pleased to raise her again she might be with me longer, and be of service, and yet go well; she readily answered,

there may be danger in that, I am now ready.

Alexander Jaffray

of *Kingswel,* in the North of *Scotland,* was born in the City of *Aberdeen* ...and as he grew in Years, he increased in a Religious Concern towards God, and those whom he did Esteem, feared him; and joyned, when young, with the *Presbyterians,* tho' Educated in another Form of Religion: But sometime after, when those People got into Rule and Government...he soon disliked them, and signified the same to some of the Chiefest among them...

After he left... for some time he was among the *Independents* and finding them also to be for setting up themselves, and persecuting others; he could no longer follow them: After this he remained in private for some Years, a Solitary Mourner, not joyning with any Professions in Religion; ...

and in his Solitary Retirement, he sought the Lord, waiting for a People who were Spiritually touch'd with a Divine Coal from the Altar, to kindle true and spiritual Sacrifices to God.

And when first he heard that God had raised up such a People in *England,* who *directed all to God's pure Light, Spirit and Grace in their own Hearts, as the most sure Teacher and Leader into all Truth, Worship and Religion,* he said, *he felt his Heart to leap within him, for Joy,* and after weighty Examination, concerning that People, called Quakers, who did Preach the Truth among them, he found His Heart and Soul united with them:

This was in the Year 1662, a time when it was as bitter a Cross, even as Death, to own them, especially to one of his Repute; and shortly after were several more Men of Note, in that Nation, Convinced of the same Way of Truth;...

He was faithful in his Testimony to the Truth to the last; and in his sickly old Age was Imprison'd many Miles from his own House for non-payment of Tithes; and this is remarkable, that a little before this Imprisonment, being near to Death, as was judged by all who saw him, he signified under his Hand, being unable to speak, by a great Sweling in his Throat,

> *that his God had yet a Service for him to do for him, in Suffering for his precious Truth, and that he was not to Dye at that time.*

He was taken Sick the latter end of the 4th Month, 1673, and during the twelve Days of his Sickness, he did give many living Testimonies to the blessed Truth, before many witnesses, both Friends and other People who did visit him..

He said, *That it was his great Joy and Comfort in that Hour, that ever he had been counted worthy to bear a Testimony to, and Suffer for that precious* Testimony of Christ Jesus...

...Sometimes being overcome in Spirit, he said,

> *Now Lord let they Servant depart in Peace, for mine Eyes Spiritually have seen, my Heart hath felt, and feeling, Shall for ever feel thy Salvation....*

77

He further said, *That the Lord had given him the Garments of Praise, instead of the Spirit of Heaviness.* Sometimes, when very Sick, he would Bless the Lord, that now fighting with a natural Death, he had not an angry God to deal with.

> *Oh!* Says he, *the sting of Death is fully gone, and Death is mine; being Reconciled to me as a sweet Passage, thro' him that lov'd me.*

Another time seeing the Candle almost out, he said,

> *My natural Life is near an end, like that Candle, for want of Nourishment, or Matter to entertain it; but in this we shall differ, that if it be let alone, that goes out with a Stink; and I shall go out with a good Savour, Praises to my God for ever.*

A little before his Breath ceased, he said, *He had been with his God, and had seen deep Things;* about which time he was *filled with the Power of God in a wonderful Manner, which much affected those present;* and in a little time after, he dyed like a Lamb, being the 6th Day of the 5th Month 1673 Aged 59 Years; and was buried in a piece of Ground, set apart, near his own House at Kingswell, the 8th of the same Month.

Thomas Upsher,   Born in the Parish of Lexden, in the *Burrough* (sic) of *Colchester,* in the County of *Essex,* ...was Religiously inclined from his Youth, often seeking the Lord for the good of his Soul, and delighted in reading the Holy Scriptures....

.....So that he was twenty Years of age when he came among the People called *Quakers,* and was a diligent Attender of the Meetings of that People for the Worship of God, waiting upon him in Silence and Retirement of Mind, for his Teaching and Counsel, until he was pleased to give unto him a Gift in the Ministry, which he received in great Humility, and entered upon his Ministry, in speaking a few Words amongst Friends, in much Fear and Tenderness, to the Comfort and Refreshment of many, and God in tender Mercy, did increase his Gift, so that he became an able Minister of the Gospel, to the turning of many from Darkness unto the Light of Christ Jesus, and in that Service he Travelled in most Parts of this Nation of *England,* and also in *Ireland.*

As he often in the time of his Health remembred and spake of his Death, so he did it in his Sickness, saying

> *I don't expect to Live long in this World, I have been preparing for a better; I do not desire to Live here on my own account; I long more and more to be at home with my God, yet I would not be of that sort, to desire my Reward before my Work is done, there is nothing here can invite my Stay, but if God*

hath further Service for me in the World, I am resigned and given up to his Will....

About the same time, several Friends being with him, he speaking of his Death, desired they might bear him Witness; saying

My Dependence Hope and Trust is only and alone in the Lord Jesus Christ; and that I don't Value myself upon any Qualification or Indowment, but lay all down at the Feet of Jesus, and am as nothing before him;

About two Days after, tho' Weak in Body, he was carried in a Coach to *Ipswich,* to the Burial of a Friend; and when he came there, he seemed very unfit for the Service of the Day, there being much People at the Burial; but the Lord strengthened him to declare, as at other times the Truth and Word of Life, for about an Hour and a Half, which much affected the People in General, and Friends, who knew his Weakness of Body, admir'd the Love and Goodness of God to him; he Pray'd also, and spake at the Grave sometime, and appeared stronger after the Meeting than before, and continued better a few Days after; but his Sickness returned again, and he was very Patient under the extremest Pains, which he said, *no Tongue could express,* desiring *to be resigned,* and the Lord Blessed him with Resignation, Faith and Patience under all....

At another time he said,

My tongue is not able to express what I feel of the
Love and Goodness of God, now when I have most
need of it, that saying used by that plain despised
People is very true, that Life is better than Words.
There is one thing I cannot find out, why the Lord
should so abound in his Love and Mercy to me, who
am unworthy of the least of his Mercy.

There was great Refreshment felt many times in being with
him in Silence, in time of his Sickness. On a first Day in the
Morning, several Friends being in his Chamber, he desired
that they might wait upon the Lord together; and the Lord
was pleased to open his Mouth, *to Praise his Holy Name....*

And he remembred the Faithful, and spoke of *their Blessed
Estate;* at the sight of which, he was even as it were in a
Rapture of Joy, praising the Lord to the Comfort of those
present; ....and taking leave of several Friends who visited
him; he said,

> *Oh! That you may so Live, that we may meet again*
> *in the Mansions of Eternal Rest.*

He remembred his dear Love to Friends everywhere; saying,

> *they are near my Life, I have true Unity with them in*
> *Spirit; ....*

About ten Days before his Death, finding himself as he
thought somewhat better, he went to the Meeting, being the
first Day of the Week, and prayed Fervently in the Forenoon
Meetng, praising the Name of the Lord, in a true Sense of
his Mercy and Goodness. But in a Day or two he alter'd

much, his Distemper prevailing upon him; he desired to be carried decently to his Grave; saying

> *I love decency, and desire to Die in great Humiliation, and commit my Spirit into the Hands of the Lord Jesus Christ.*

And about the time of his Death, he was in a Heavenly Frame of Spirit, and spake of a Glorious Meeting, and said, *The Lord in the Riches of his Mercy, will keep all them that Trust in him, under all their Tryals to the end.*

And so he departed this Life, the tenth of the eighth Month, 1704 Aged thirty two Years two Months. He left behind him three Children, and his Wife big with Child, who in the time of his Sickness was much indispos'd, which was an Addition to his Exercise.

Reflection

In dialogue with those present, the dying one intends to offer comfort by stressing that s/he is eager to go. The stance they convey over and over again is that they are looking forward to release; in their passage towards death, they will become free of suffering. They also stress the need to do the work of repentance in good time.

There is often a sequence when those by the deathbed are beseeching the dying one not to go. 'Thou must give me freely up' says Deborah Bell, yet her husband is portrayed as longing to hold on to her, asking 'if she had not rather live with me a little longer'.

It is also true that some authors found death less welcoming – and of course it is certainly possible that the saying, as quoted, followed a series of other stages expressing a much greater willingness to die.

What remains intriguing, reading these sayings today, is the question of how they would have been read – and heard - at the time. In those we have just read, the speaker is heard on several different occasions, over several days. Their sayings are presented as a series of addresses to an audience.

Their value to those of us hearing them three centuries later has to do with an invitation. It seems to me that we are being invited to share in the experience of the speaker, as if we were travelling with them on a journey towards our own death - and towards our acceptance of it. The obstacles of certain language may be in our way, but (if we listen) we can find in them something to speak to us.

The dying Friend nearly always has advice to give both to those at the time, and to us who come later. "Live well in the faith as I have done, and you can die well too" with the extra message: "I go willingly; I am not afraid; I want to go."

With this comes another question. After all this activity to record and circulate the last words of certain Friends, once they stopped publishing these 'dying sayings', how did Friends continue the practice of recording their words?

Testimonies to the grace of God

Betty Hagglund offers an answer. Reprints of the bound 'Piety Promoted' volumes appeared several times, until 1838. Meanwhile, from 1813 until 1920, a new and different system of Quaker record began appearing in the form of the *Annual Monitor* with a full list of British Quakers who died each year, compiled from information supplied by Monthly Meetings. This at least gave a much greater number of those recorded (over 20,000 in the period) but with only fuller information on a small proportion of them.

At the same time, another effort was evidently going into the collation and publication of a different set of records: a series of reports of Friends' persecutions from the beginning of the movement in the 1650s until the Toleration Act in 1689:

what came to be published in 1753 as Joseph Besse's 'Sufferings of early Quakers'. For Friends today the facsimile reproductions of these volumes are a wonderful resource, allowing us access to vital parts of our history. [3]

During some of the same period (between 1740 and 1872) Friends were also encouraged to a habit of compiling retrospective Testimonies concerning 'Ministers deceased' which was followed (in 1861) by those for any Friend whose life had been 'marked by conspicuous service to God and the church'.

Later, in 1931 London Yearly Meeting issued an invitation to any Monthly Meeting to also to issue testimonies 'to the grace of God as shown in the life' of a deceased Friend. This time there was guidance, specifying that it should not be a eulogy or an obituary: a guidance which still continues the same invitation:

> The possibility of writing a testimony concerning the life and service of a deceased Friend has been a valued part of our tradition. A testimony should not be a formal obituary or eulogy but should record in thankfulness the power of divine grace in human life. [4]

Area (formerly Monthly) Meetings take responsibility for composing a testimony, send the result to Britain Yearly

[3] Hagglund (2013) p486, Besse (1753)
[4] Quaker Faith and Practice, Fifth edition (2013) 4.27

Meeting's staff, who then publish those received in an 'epistles and testimonies' document for that year's 'Yearly Meeting in session'. Clerks then select a few to be read aloud at that event – attended, these days, by more than a thousand Friends. At the nine or ten of these events at which I have been present, I have been part of the throng listening to such testimonies being read to us from the platform, and felt as if we were celebrating the spirit of the deceased Friend among us. At the local level, I have been part of the process of generating two such testimonies.

However, neither the large public reading nor the small-scale discernment has ever quite matched for me the special character of the 'dying sayings' collection: with its commitment to capture, however imperfectly, the *words of the Friend themselves*, in their last hours, framed within a portrait of their spiritual presence among us.

6 MEANINGS

The work has confused me, certainly; but it has also recharged me, as a Quaker. On the one hand it has led me to learn more about the roots of our movement. At the same time, it has inspired me to rediscover its fruits - and to appreciate their range and diversity.

In gathering and putting these sayings together I have wanted to untangle the ways in which they might have had meaning for their authors, editors, and audiences of the time. As to their meaning for readers in the very different world of communications that we inhabit now: only you can say.

The three final authors I have chosen for particular reasons: Priscilla Richards, for her experience as the child of parents with mixed feelings about Quakers; John Tomkins, for his delight in service and the number of times he speaks of his love for others; and Tacey Davis, whose death was plainly a difficult and painful one, but who found the words to show others the divine assistance she expects to be given.

Priscilla Richards	1680-1704 (24)	Liskeard, Cornwall
John Tomkins	1643-1706 (73)	London
Tacey Davis	d. 1705 (90)	Welshpool

Priscilla Richards Daughter of *John Richards* of *Howsey* near *Liskard,* in the County of *Cornwall,* and of *Priscilla* his Wife, was Born at *Liskard,* the 18th of the sixth Month, 1680 and tho' Educated in her Fathers Family, who were mostly Strangers to the living way of Truth, now in this our Age revealed; only her Mother frequented the Meetings of the People called *Quakers;*

yet did this Young Maiden begin according to the Advice of the Wise-Man (sic), to *Remember her Creator in the Days of her Youth,* and did not only come to the Meetings of the said People, but she turned with her Heart to the Lord, and as she came towards seventeen Years of Age; she grew in the *Fear of God and in Plainness and Solidity...*and in all her Deportment, and was greatly in Love with the Company of the best Friends, to whom she also became very acceptable....

She was scarcely twenty Years of Age, when she was visited with some Infirmities of Body, which still drove her *nearer the Lord;* and altho' she met with some Exercises grievous to her tender Spirit, yet she was *resigned to the Will of God.*

About the beginning of the Year 1704 It was perceived by some Symptoms, that her Distemper tended to a Dropsy, in which abundance of care, both of Parents and able Physicians was used; yet her Disease increased, so that it was Apparent some Months before she died, that there was little or no hopes of her Recovery; which she foresaw, yet was very well satisfied and resigned to the Will of God, in which she had Peace and great quietness of Mind, and would often testifie as much to her Mother, and those about her, as well as Friends, who frequently visited her; for she having her Affections drawn out of the world, it became easie to her to leave it.

In a letter to a particular Friend, who married her near Relation, written about fourteen Days before she died, she says thus

> *Dear Cousin, I should have given an account of my Sickness, but exceeding Illness hindered me, and my Mother, what with Sorrow for me, and want of time, occasioned the same neglect; I am now very ill, being swoln all over my Body, except my Hands and Arms, and am Scarcely able to walk the Chamber without help;*
> *But I am freely given up to the will of my Heavenly Father, whether for Life or Death; I should be glad to see any of you here, for my time in this World is not like to be long; I have been a little better at my Heart this four or five Days, but how it will please the Lord to deal with me I know not; my Dear Love is to thee, thy Wife and Children, wishing you Health and Peace in this Life, and Happiness in the World to come, being Dear Cousin thine Affectionate, &c, P.R.....*

This was written in a time of great Weakness of Body, but her Spirit was strong in the Lord, having kept the Faith, and by it was made a Conqueror.......

On the 14th of the 7th month, being sensibly weakened, and feeling the Approaches of Death, she said, *Come, Come, Come, why so long;* and in a very little time after, called out, *Lord Jesus receive my Spirit,* and presently breathed forth her last, according to her Prayer to the Lord, that she might not go stupefied out of the World, for she died in full Understanding, and Soundness of Mind, and is gone to Rest in the Lord, Blessed by his Name for Ever.

On the 18th of the seventh Month 1704 her Body was decently Buried from her Fathers House in Friends Burying-Ground, in the Parish of *Liskard.*

John Tomkins, as he grew in Years, he grew in Grace, and in the Knowledge of our Lord and Saviour Jesus Christ. And being faithful unto the Lord, he was pleased to put him into the Ministry, and committed to him the Word of *Reconciliation,* and made him a skilful Minister, for his time, in the Word of Life: ....He was filled with such a holy Zeal for the Name and Truth of God, as was accompanied with Knowledge, and was well acquainted with our Christian Discipline, and careful that it might be maintained, greatly desiring where any Professing Truth, walked not according to it, that they might be admonished and reproved...

One asking him how he did, he replied, *Very weak, but I am willing to die, and leave this troublesome World, if the Lord sees it meet to remove me at this time.*

And lying on his Bed very weak, he declared to Friends, then present, very fervently for some time, concerning the Work of the Lord, and the Prosperity of his Truth in the Earth; ... and to be of one Heart and Mind, and that the Work of the Lord should go forward in the Earth, and his Truth prosper over all the Kingdoms of it, and many Nations should be gathered to it.

He also said, *I believe the Lord will bless his People, and carry on the Work he hath begun in the Earth: And it is my Faith, that the time will come, that the Wicked shall be as few, as the Righteous are now: But there is much to be* purged out of the Church; there is much Pride and Superfluity to be done away.

And again said, *I have seen great things since my Sickness; Things which I think not lawful to be spoken.*

Much good Counsel and Advice drop'd from him, at sundry Times, that was not taken down in Writing, which he gave at times to his Friends and Relations about him,

And often said to his Wife, *My dear, grieve not, thou must not grieve; I want to be where the weary are at rest, and where the Wicked cease from troubling. I want to be Dissolved, that I may be with the Lord Jesus Christ; the Lord will provide for thee and thy Children. He hath said,* Let their Widows trust in me, and I will take care of their Fatherless Children.

When he was asked, If he desired to see his Youngest Child (he being some Miles distant) he answered, *He is Young, and hath little Knowledge of me, I commit him to the Great God, he will take care of him.* He spake this with more than ordinary Sedateness, adding, *I am not afraid of Death, I have sought the Honour of God in my day, and my Reward is with him, The Lord hath been very good to me in this Sickness, I can say with the* Psalmist, He had made my Bed in my Sickness. *I have many sweet seasons from the Lord in the Night when I cannot Sleep: Oh! The Love of the Lord Jesus Christ is great to Mankind.*

The Lord visited me in my tender Years, and I have feared him from my childhood. I have delighted to wipe the Shoes of those that Preach the Gospel, when I was a Boy: And since I have been a Man, I have taken more delight in serving the Lord, his Church and People, than in getting of Worldly Riches. I love the Poor, and have loved to serve them, and to visit them in their Afflictions. Remember my Love to the Poor in the Quarter where I dwell.

I love the Ministry, I have a valuable esteem for the Ministers, and pray God Purge and Sanctifie them, that they may go before the Flock. And I pray God to bless the Young Generation of Ministers, that are coming up, and make them skilful in the work, that they may divide the Word aright, that like the Benjamites (sic) of Old, they may shoot an Arrow [or fling a Stone] to an Hairs Breadth.

He died the 12th of the 7th Month, 1706. Aged about 43 Years.

Tacey Davis, Wife of *Richard Davis*, of *Welsh-Pool* in *Montgomery-shire*, she formerly dwelt in *London*, but after her Marriage, removed with her Husband to *Pool* abovesaid, where were few or no Friends at that time, which was about the Year 1659.

She had a publick Testimony in Meetings, and was Instrumental to bring many to the Truth, and was an Entertainer with her Husband of Strangers, and a Nursing Mother to those in Prison, for the Testimony of a good Conscience, and they lived together to old Age; she cheerfully went thro' the various Exercise and hard Sufferings, which attended in those Days them that professed the blessed Truth; she was taken Sick the 29th of the second Month, 1705, and had been at a Meeting the same Day, which was kept at their House about forty years.

After the extremity of her Pain was somewhat abated, she said, *People don't think it so hard to Dye, as I find it*, and Pray'd *thus*.

> *O Lord accept of me in thy well-beloved Son Christ Jesus; I have loved thee with all my Soul, and spirit, I have kept thy Commandments; Oh! Lord bless my Family, with all Heavenly Blessings, grant to them that they may live in thy Fear;*

She said to the Servant Maid, who was not a Friend,

> *Remember thy Creator in the days of thy Youth; leave off thy Vanity before such a Day as this*

overtake thee; I have nothing to do but to strive with this natural Distemper, I loved the Lord in my young Days, and he kept me from many Evils, and when he was pleased to make known his blessed Truth to me, he helped me to work out my Salvation with fear and trembling, that Work I have not to do now, the Lord Jesus Christ did it in me, and for me,

upon which, the Maid wept much; at another time, Pain coming on her, she said,

I feel I am of a strong Constitution, and that Nature would not yield to my Distemper

and prayed fervently, saying, *come Lord Jesus Christ, come quickly, and put an end to my Pain, Lord I long to be with thee for ever;* another time she pray'd,

O Lord, I am the workmanship of thy Hands, thou hast often helped me in the time of need, for thy Names Sake, help me now in the time of my distress, thou art my God, my Hope, and my Help; I will trust in thee, Oh my God! Oh! God hasten thy coming for thy son Christ Jesus sake;

another time, she said to her Husband *I have done too little for the Lord;* her Husband put her in mind of her many former Services, and particularly visiting his Servants when in Prison for Christ's sake, feeding them when Hungry, entertaining Strangers, and when Sick, very tender in helping them, etc.

She replied,

> *all this too little to do for the Lord Jesus Sake, who hath loved us, we must not depend upon these things, but we must depend and trust in our Lord and Saviour Jesus Christ; and when we have done all, let us account our selves unprofitable Servants, for we have done but that which was our Duty;*

and a little before she died, she desired her Husband to

> *Praise the Lord with her, for all his Mercys,*
> *and at this time, that I feel his living Presence, to my great Comfort;*

and she Prayed her self saying,

> *O Lord, thou hast been a Father to me, thou hast kept me from Evil, and now I trust in thy great Name, that thou will not forsake me for thy Son Christ Jesus Sake,* take me to thy Self.

And she was heard; about the sixth Hour in the Afternoon, on the first Day of the third Month, 1705 the Lord in his Love and Mercy took her to himself, in great quietness, and peace of spirit, in about the 90th Year of her Age.

Reflection

The Quaker message

Of all the authors, Tacey Davis – in combination with her attentive husband – seems to me to express most eloquently the female heart within the Christian idea of the divine. The Lord features frequently in her words, but (again, to me) without any sense of a dominant, all-knowing masculine presence. 'The Lord Jesus' is the light in her soul, showing her a loving God taking her in 'in great quietness'.

After a long life of 'labours in the gospel', she had still felt she had not done enough for the sake of that light, despite her loving self (or husband) reminding her of her many efforts. She now knows that God's 'hope' and 'help', in which she has tried to trust all her life, is now waiting for her in death.

Today, in our Quaker meetings for worship, there is variety in how much different Friends may feel led to minister out loud. Years and years may pass and one Friend who joins the worship faithfully every week may never speak. And then – as early Friends would say - their 'tongue may be loosened'; the spirit moves, and they are on their feet.

The authors of these sayings had to speak up in much harder conditions. For those in the mid-1650s and onwards caught up in the excitement of the live performances by Quaker ministers, the experience of worship being proposed must have been new and dangerous. For those of us discovering Quaker worship in the early 21st century it may be strangely calming. The Anglican services of my childhood had involved changes of physical position to think about – kneeling, standing, sitting, etc – prayers to say, hymns to sing and a priest in front of us to listen to. Sitting among others with heads bowed in Quaker meeting for an hour with just the quiet and occasional unplanned speaker was at first a simple matter.

In time, I was accepted into membership, served in different roles in Local, Area and Yearly meetings and life became more complicated. Over the years I have learned about the discipline and (like John Tomkins) came to love it. I also learned that it takes work. There are disagreements to resolve and weariness involved. (Why would it be easy?) Spending time among the lives of the people who got it all started has meant finding a kind of unity with them and their 'labours in the gospel'.

The language
More specifically, I have noticed three words of which the 'dying sayings' collection refreshes our usual understandings.

(1) Happiness

A 'good' life as a means to a good death is a familiar idea. The surprise I found was how often editors and authors spoke of 'happiness' rather than goodness: for instance, James Baines who died in a 'happy and most blessed condition'; Elizabeth Barker saying 'I am happy' in reply to a relative grieving at her departure (in Chapter 3); and William Stovey, who declared he was *pleased, to leave this World, in Expectation of a far greater Happiness in that which is to come* (Chapter 4).

For the collection editors, piety should consist in a 'holy happiness' and this condition be not confined to the few, but to all who obey the calling:

> 'Wonderful hath been the Love of God unto the Children of Men, and Various have been the Methods, whereby he hath given Demonstrations of it;...For his Goodness hath been always so Plentifully extended, and also in such an Indulgent Manner, as if his Happiness was not compleat, unless Mankind did partake of it....For we have also, in this our Day, been Honoured with a Visitation from Heaven; a High and Holy Calling indeed; a Call to be *Holy,* in order to be *Happy;* But few have Obeyed, tho' Christ himself hath Called by his Spirit....' (pp2)

It's a lovely, joyful view – but also a challenge. For the founding Friends, truly pious lives and sayings should be a living witness to the difficult claims of a Christian faith. It was not enough to 'profess' the doctrines of the Christian Religion. The path to piety is only truly to be found in 'a holy life and a right ordered Conversation'. No amount of virtue based only on text will suffice; it is the 'doing part' that matters:

> `The Knowledge only of what is right and good, the Profession thereof, or being Educated in the Doctrines of the Christian Religion, will not Intitle any to Eternal Happiness, if the doing Part be wanting; for Piety is not Promoted by a bare Notion and Profession, or saying Prayers, bearing Sermons or Declarations, but by a holy Life, and a right ordered Conversation.' (pp4)

Within the Friends' central purpose - to promote piety - there is then an idea of union with divine bliss.

(2) Illiteracy

At the heart of my interest in these sayings is a fascination with authorship. It all began with years of work in adult literacy education in the 1970s and 80s – a time when, in Britain, there was public alarm at the supposed level of illiteracy in our population. At that time, some of us developed a set of ideas to suggest another way of thinking about it: more to do with context and relationship than with skills and levels. Those who came to us with a sense of shame about their own skills in reading and writing had much to teach us and *authorship* became a key idea in our work together. We developed a scribal approach that enabled someone to bypass anxieties about being 'wrong' in how they wrote to become confident in creating their own expression.[1]

Many years later I discovered how Quakers draft minutes and expect the meeting as a whole to share responsibility for deciding whether the written record is acceptable or not. The clerk (often with a second Friend at her side) reads out the draft then and there to those present, who accept it and/or offer amendments. Authorship of the finished text is then collective.[2] I witnessed the potential power of these writing ways. The day I came away from my first Quaker Meeting for Worship for Business was my first step in becoming a convinced Quaker.

In Chapter 2 we saw how Priscilla Cotton vigorously challenged the conventional view of lettered learning: celebrating instead the capacity for a spiritual wisdom that transcends text. After too much in our culture claiming that the only proper intelligence is the kind that shows itself in correct and/or clever writing, I love this view.

---

[1] Mace (1992) p16-22 and (2002)
[2] Ibid (2012).

Among the authors of the 'dying sayings' there are few references to someone being of limited education; and far from judging these also to be limited in their understanding, rather the opposite is often expressed. William Wilson, for example, was clearly thought to have value that went beyond mere schooling: being

> a man of an Innocent Life; and little of Outward Learning, and yet God was pleased to Teach him Himself, and called him to bear a Testimony to his Name, and he did it Faithfully; not only in many parts of this Nation, but also in Germany and several times in Scotland. A Man of a lowly and meek Spirit, Upright and just among his Neighbours, which caused them often to commit their Matters in Difference to his Arbitration....

Perhaps of particular interest is the attribute given to Edward Burrough (Chapter 3), a leading early Quaker if ever there was one, described as 'a Man of no great Learning, which Men so much Admire, yet [having] the Tongue of the Learned.'

In Chapter 4, we saw how John Carlisle, after years as an active travelling Quaker preacher, was described as 'illiterate as to outward Learning', but yet differently literate 'in his Doctrine, and Testimony' - opening for others 'the Scriptures of Truth, by the Assistance of that Holy Spirit that gave them forth'. Notably, he evidently also knew the value of mingling the use of 'a few Words' with 'Silence.... To feel an increase and Growth in the Vertue of Truth' among his listeners.

(3) Savour (and savoury)

These days, this word usually refers to taste of food. Evidently early Friends (and perhaps others of the same period) enjoyed it as having a spiritual meaning – as I do too.

In these pages we have met three people said to possess the quality: William Gibson having 'a memorial 'of *good Savour* in those Parts'; John Carlisle 'having born an innocent Testimony for Truth in his Generation, and left a good *Savour* behind him' and – most memorably – Alexander Jaffray (Chapter 5) speaking of his 'natural life' nearing its end,

> 'like that Candle, for want of Nourishment, or Matter to entertain it; but in this we shall differ, that if it be let alone, that goes out with a Stink; and I shall go out with a good Savour'.

From elsewhere in the Piety Promoted collection, Richard Samble (pp2) is described as being 'a sweet Savour in his Day'; his Wife not remembering ever hearing him *speak an unsavoury word* in twelve years of their marriage.

....

There are of course mysteries that remain with this work. One of them is the gap (in some, of as much as 35 years) between the publication dates of 1701or 1702 and the dates of death of some of the authors. John Tomkins had been collecting and in some cases himself recording sayings over a considerable period. What might have been his sources? and what was it that made the task of collecting and editing them so important? From the other volumes of the 'Piety promoted' collection answers will emerge. What is clear is that anyone deciding to join the 'people call'd Quakers' at that time was choosing a new life – and the possibility of being landed in a lot of trouble. It seems clear that a primary impact of these 'testimonies' may well have been to strengthen their resolve.

In some sense, that is how I have experienced myself the impact of the piety being promoted. Humbled both by the quality and quantity of the witness they were making, I am compelled to feel renewed by the passion that moved them.

APPENDIX (1) Barbados

How did Alice Curwen (Chapter 1) and her husband come to be travelling to Barbados?

In 'Dying sayings' I came across a number of men and women who, in the 1650s, included this West Indian island in their long journeys of mission. Further research revealed more. First 'settled' as a British colony in 1627, Barbados was the destination of many Quakers between the 1650s and 1670s, some time before their better-known settlement in Philadelphia was founded in 1682 (where by 1690 William Penn was able to record the arrival there of ten slaveships from the West Indies).

Among the first Quaker missionaries there were Mary Fisher (then aged 22) and Mary Austin who landed in 1655[5] and went on to make several successful converts. So Alice and her husband were following in their footsteps. As to how these white English Quakers and the people already living there got on together, we can begin to imagine from research, particularly that of historian Katharine Gerbner, who has made a study of this period[6] and who reports that

---

[5] Moore (2013) p20
[6] Gerbner (2018)

'Two decades on, thousands of Quakers were living in Barbados, all but four of whom were slaveowners.' [7]

Along with other studies, hers has also documented slave ownership among the first English Quakers migrants to Philadelphia from Barbados, where enslaved Africans had become the major labour force.

When George Fox visited Quakers in the colonies, Barbados was his first stop. It has been noted that he did not at that time call for an end to slavery. His concern rather was that Friends should ensure they worshipped together with the slaves in their households. It was that which led 17th century Quakers there to be seen to be radical.

By the 18th and 19th centuries, Quakers certainly played a major part in the abolitionist movement, Gerbner reminds us: but (as she pointed out in the lecture I was able to watch), that should not allow us to forget those who came before.

---

[7] *(2nd April 2019 lecture* at the Museum of the American Revolution 'Slavery and Quakers in 17th Century Barbados' https://www.c-span.org/video/?459546-1/slavery-quakers-17th-century-barbados : *accessed 1/7/20*

APPENDIX (2) Scribal partnerships

One of the better known 17th century Friends providing a scribal service was Anne Downer Whitehead. Usually known in her adult life by her married name as Anne (or Ann) Whitehead, the name given in 'Quaker Faith and Practice' is her unmarried one: Anne Downer, as in the introduction to the passage for which she served as scribe:

> *This statement comes in George Fox's letter to ministers, which he sent in 1656 when he was in prison in Launceston in Cornwall. It was written down for him by Ann Downer (1624-1686), who had walked from London to help him. Later she was a very influential Friend in the women's meetings in London. George Fox wrote:.......*[1]

From her 'dying saying' in Part 1 of the first volume there is a fuller picture of the story behind this activity. Ann not only made the distance to Cornwall to visit Friends in Launceston prison, Cornwall; she ministered along the way – and in that Journey, as one testifier recorded after her death,

> 'convinced many People, and some of Account; and in her Return, did Confirm and Establish several that were new Convinced'.

Not only, then, did Ann have the ability to be a useful secretary, but she must also have been a persuasive preacher

---

[1] Quaker Faith and Practice 19.32

– with, according to other evidence, a 'readiness in accounts and disposing of it more than many, for abilities therein exceeded most'.. very much part of the Swarthmoor Hall arrangements for the support of Friends suffering fines and imprisonment.[2] And going on to give service in time of plague and fire in London in the 1660s. [3]

George Fox's letter to ministers or Epistle is best known today for the ending: 'answering that of God in everyone'.   Heard spoken aloud, the whole must have had a powerful effect. In the process of its composition in the prison cell we can imagine that Fox and Anne tested the draft out loud - as other Friends, elsewhere, would have heard it in the weeks or months that followed its distribution.

Reading it on the page, we can still sense its power, as a declaration and call to the faithful.   The following is the (almost) full text of these words as they appear in *Quaker Faith and. Practice*:

---

[2] Trevett, (1995) p71
[3] ibid p117

"Friends,

In the power of life and wisdom, and dread of the Lord God of life, and heaven, and earth, dwell; that in the wisdom of God over all ye may be preserved, and be a terror to all the adversaries of God, and a dread, answering that of God in them all, spreading the Truth abroad, awakening the witness, confounding deceit, gathering up out of transgression into the life, the covenant of light and peace with God
Let all nations hear the word by sound or writing. Spare no place, spare not tongue nor pen, but be obedient to the Lord God and go through the world and be valiant for the Truth upon earth; tread and trample all that is contrary under.

Keep in the wisdom of God that spreads over all the earth, the wisdom of the creation, that is pure. Live in it; that is the word of the Lord God to you all, do not abuse it; and keep down and low; and take heed of false joys that will change.

......And this is the word of the Lord God to you all, and a charge to you all in the presence of the living God: be patterns, be examples in all countries, places, islands, nations, wherever you come, that your carriage and life may preach among all sorts of people, and to them; then you will come to walk cheerfully over the world, answering that of God in everyone."

We have become used to thinking of this Epistle as the words of George Fox and, since Ann was apparently an experienced shorthand writer, that could be true: she could have taken them down verbatim.

Research suggests there is a spectrum in the role of scribe across cultures and periods, ranging from a monastic copyist to co-author[4]. I'm inclined to see Anne in the latter role: encouraging and suggesting, listening and repeating back phrases: the kind of scribe who could have been helpful with the composition, on an equal footing; a service which George, worn out by conditions in prison, might have welcomed.

However it happened, it follows that the authorship of this passage might better be recorded as being joint: possibly in alphabetical order of their first names – so that the quoted words would be introduced not with 'George Fox wrote' but rather with; "Anne Downer and George Fox wrote:..."

---

[4] Mace (2002) pp 124-128

APPENDIX (3) The Collection

The total 'Piety Promoted' collection was published between 1701 and 1796. It is easy to get a bit confused with its Volumes and Parts, not least because each of them went into more than one edition. In the list on the next page I have shown how the system changed from 'part' to 'volume' when it came to number (4)

The focus of this book is on Volume (1). Consisting of three Parts, this is the one I have read most thoroughly, having been able to borrow this copy from my own Area Meeting library. Only by physically visiting the Quaker reference libraries at Woodbrooke in Birmingham and Friends House in London could I (or anyone else) have had access to the others –they being scrupulously cared for in locked cupboards by the staff in both organisations; brought out to a library table only by prior request.

The best guide I found to the whole collection turned out to have been written by the editor of the last volume, Joseph Gurney Bevan, published as part of his introduction to the 1810 edition of parts previously published. The following is a summary of the dates and numbers of sayings in each, together with his notes on two of the editors, provided by his 'historical account of the preceding parts or volumes, and of their several compilers and editors'[8] [9]

Vol/year	Number/names	Editor
Vol 1 (pt1) 1701	- 59	John Tomkins
(pt2) 1701	- 48	John Tomkins
(pt3) 1701	- 48	John Tomkins with Christopher Meidel
Vol 4 - 1711	- 54	John Field
Vol 5 - 1717	- 57	John Field
Vol 6 - 1723	- 29	John Field
Vol 7 - 1740	- 32	John Bell
Vol 8 - 1774	- 66	Thomas Wagstaffe
Vol 9 - 1796	- 66	Thomas Wagstaffe

Editors

The first editor of the collection, John Tomkins (1663-1706) was the child of Quakers. His father died when he was very young; and, as he grew up, he not only assisted his mother in her business, but was helpful to another family of children which she had by a second husband, who survived her and

---

[8] The three parts in Volume 1 are numbered separately in parentheses. Subsequent volumes are numbered singly as in the originals.
[9] In addition to these volumes, Joseph Gurney Bevan reports that in 1760 the London printer Mary Hinde published a selection of 72 individual narratives and sayings translated into French by Claude Gay.

afterwards fell into poverty. His death at the age of 43 probably took place at the house of his friend Christopher Meidel.

While Christopher Meidel's name is not mentioned in Joseph Gurney Bevan's historical note, a scholarly article tells us more[10]. He was among the first Norwegian contacts with British Quakers when some of them were in Norway. His father, a shipowner, travelled to England in that capacity. He himself, born 1659, grew up as a Lutheran. Coming to England as Chaplain to Prince George of Denmark the husband of Queen Anne, he became preacher to the Danish church in London; and afterwards pastor to an independent congregation in Nightingale Lane, East Smithfield. He was convinced and joined the Society of Friends in 1699, going on to translate a number of Quaker papers into Norwegian.

In 1705, when he was preaching Quakerism in the open streets he was arrested by soldiers, imprisoned in Newgate and released in 1706 - the date of his preface-writing for *Piety Promoted*, after his friend's death.[11] A year later he was in prison again (in Launceston Castle) charged with having 'disturbed the priest in his ministerial function'.

---

[10] Cadbury (1941)

113

Well known as the author of many short pieces, several of them controversial, John Field took up the editorial work for the Piety collection, producing in 1711 a fourth volume (with a long preface by an anonymous writer) and in 1717 a fifth, with two more to follow. (In the register of the Quarterly Meeting he was described as Haberdasher, but Joseph Gurney Bevan doubts this, noting 'I have heard that his trade was a woollen-draper.')

For many years, there were no more volumes, until a seventh appeared in 1740, edited by John Bell, containing a long preface by him. After settling in Bradford, he and his wife Deborah had moved to London in 1715. Both were active travellers in the ministry. Among other names in this volume is that of Deborah herself, whose 'dying saying' (featured in Chapter 5) was first published in 1740.

Several years passed before, in 1774, Thomas Wagstaffe added an 8th volume, containing sixty-six accounts of deceased friends.

'Eight volumes having thus been presented to Friends and finding a ready demand' (writes Joseph Gurney Bevan) the work 'again became scarce' until, in 1789, John Kendall of Colchester published a revised edition of the whole with preface, printed by James Phillips (who had succeeded Mary Hinde as printer in the Society).

Purposes

All the editors wrote copious introductions. To summarise their purpose in collecting and publishing these notes and sayings of individual Friends, here is how three of them expressed it. In his preface to 1ˢᵗ part John Tomkins explains the special value, as he saw it, of these being their last words:

> And having in the Course of my Reading, met with many excellent Sayings of our dying Friends, that afforded me much Satisfaction of Mind, as aforesaid, I have Collected some of them together, for the Benefit of others; knowing, that usually the Words of dying Persons makes deeper Impression on the Minds of Men, than words spoken at other times."

In his preface to Part 3 Christopher Meidel makes a special case for the need to promote piety 'in such an Age as this, wherein Impiety is so sensibly Promoted, not only by the Notoriously Prophane, but also by the Presumptuously Careless Professors of Christianity'. 'Dying words', he writes, 'even of the worst of Men and Malefactors...[are already being used as] a Warning against Vice, and Incentive to Vertue'. How much greater, he says, is the benefit of 'the Dying Words of the Righteous (whose Death is precious in the Eyes of the Lord)'.

In John Field's words, these sayings gave expression to the difficult effort required to live up to the claims of a Christian faith. For in his view and that of the other founding Friends of Truth, no amount of outward knowledge or 'profession' of the 'doctrines of the Christian Religion' would entitle anyone to 'eternal happiness'. For them, the only true path to piety was by living a *holy life*:

> `The Knowledge only of what is right and good, the Profession thereof, or being Educated in the Doctrines of the Christian Religion, will not Intitle any to Eternal Happiness, if the doing Part be wanting; for Piety is not Promoted by a bare Notion and Profession, or saying Prayers, bearing Sermons or Declarations, but by a holy Life, and a right ordered Conversation.'

Printers

In his decision to include the account of Andrew Sowle in Part 1 of the first volume, John Tomkins gave his daughter the chance to ensure her father would be remembered, too: his commitment to 'the Truth' - having enabled him

> 'with much Cheerfulness to undergo those manifold Afflictions and Persecutions, with which he was exercised...being for several Years together in continual danger; his House being often searched and his Printing Materials, as Press, Letter, &c, as often broken to pieces, and taken away....During which time, tho' he met with great Losses, and had at one time, by his Adversaries, about a Thousand Reams of Printed Books taken from him; yet he was never heard to complain, but would say, *He was glad he had*

anything to lose for Truth, and that the Lord had made him worthy to be a Sufferer for it.'

'T.Sowle' or **Tace Sowle** (1665-1749) had served her printing apprenticeship with her father, taking on his mantle as a principal Quaker publisher when his eyesight went and carrying on the business for some fifty years after his death – during what were very likely still risky times for printers.

According to Gil Skidmore, [12]

> 'Tace considerably increased the number of Quaker books published by the firm and eventually became virtually the official Quaker printer. She sometimes had more of an eye to business than some Friends appreciated, often printing more copies of a book than she had been asked for if she thought that there was a demand, until her paymasters, Six Weeks Meeting, ordered her to stop.

> In 1734 she was asked to join the Women's Meeting of London, probably so that they could draw on her business acumen, as Tace was never a public Friend.'.

As to the origin of her first name, a note from *Quakers in Publishing* offers a thoughtful observation. Coming from the Latin *taceo*, meaning 'I am silent', it awards her with a certain

---

[12] Skidmore (1998)

power in the publishing process. As they point out: 'we have no writings of her own, but her skill made it certain that other Quaker writers were heard'[13].

She is remembered today by a fund which aims to enable the publication of Quaker works in the developing world.[14]

---

[13] http://www.quakerquip.com/about/
[14] Carn (2011) and www.quakerquip.com

Bibliography

Angell, S and Dandelion, P (2013) *The Oxford handbook of Quaker Studies Oxford* University Press

Besse, J ([1753] 1998-2000)_*Sufferings of Early Quakers, West Midlands 1650-1690),* (and 6 other volumes) William Sessions Trust/Sessions Book Trust

Booy, D (2004) *Autobiographical writings by Early Quaker Women* Routledge

Brayshaw, A.Neave ([1921] 1982) *The Quakers: their story and message* William Sessions Book Trust

Cadbury, H (1941) 'Christopher Meidel and the First Norwegian Contacts with Quakerism' *The Harvard Theological Review* Vol. 34, No. 1 (Jan. 1941), pp.7-23, https://www.jstor.org/stable/1508195,

Carn, T (2011) 'An early Quaker woman printer', *The Friend,* 4 February p12

Gerbner, K (2018) *Christian Slavery Conversion and Race in the Protestant Atlantic World.* University of Pennsylvania Press

Gill, C and Hobby, E (2013) *'This I warn you in love': witness of some early Quaker women,* The Kindlers

Graves M PP (2013) 'Ministry and preaching' in: Angell and Dandelion (p277-291)

Hagglund, B (2013) 'Quakers and print culture' in: Angell and Dandelion (p477-492)

Lampen, D (1978) *Facing death* Quaker Home Service

Mace, J (1992) *Talking about literacy: principles and practice of adult literacy education* Routledge

Mace, J (2002) *The give and take of writing: scribes, literacy and everyday life* National Institute of Adult and Continuing Education

Mace, J (2012) *God and decision making: a Quaker approach* Quaker Books

Mombo, E and Nyiramana, C (2016) *Mending broken hearts, rebuilding shattered lives: Quaker peacebuilding in East and Central Africa,* Quaker Books

Moore, R (2013) 'Seventeenth century context and Quaker beginnings' in: Angell and Dandelion (p13-29)

Peters, K (2005) *Print culture and the early Quakers.* Cambridge University Press

Roads, J (2019) *Sweetness of Unity - three hundred years of Quaker minuting,* Judith Road

Shipler Chico, L (2014) *This light that pushes me: stories of African Peacebuilders* Quaker Books

Skidmore, G (1998) *Dear Friends and Sisters,* Sowle Press

Spencer, C.D (2013).'Quakers in theological context', in Angell and Dandelion (p141-157)

Spufford, M (1981) *Small books and pleasant histories: popular fiction and readership in 17th century England,* Cambridge University Press

Spufford, M (ed) (1995) *The world of rural dissenters 1520-1725,* Cambridge University Press

Taylor, Ernest (1988 [1947]) *The valiant sixty,* William Sessions Book Trust

Trevett, D (1995 [1991]) *Women and Quakerism in the 17th century* Sessions Book Trust

Vincent, D (2000) *The rise of mass literacy: reading and writing in modern Europe* Polity Press

Watt, Tessa (1993) *Cheap print and popular piety, 1550-1640* Cambridge University Press

Names index from the three Parts
of *Piety Promoted*, Volume 1
John Tomkins
edition published 1703.

(dates and ages at death deduced from individual 'sayings')

Part 1

Name		death	Age
John	Audland	1663	34
Christopher	Bacon	1656	55
Richard	Baker	1697	
David	Barclay	1686	76
Giles	Barnardiston	1680	
Robert	Barrow	1697	
William	Bayley	1675	
Sarah	Beck	1679	
Tudor	Brain	1696	17
Elizabeth	Braithwait	1684	17
Joseph	Briggins	1675	13
Edward	Burrough	1662	27
Sarah	Cam	1682	9
John	Camm	1656	52
William	Coal	1678	
Josiah	Coale	1668	
Stephen	Crisp	1692	64
Joseph F*	Crowland	1682	
Alice	Curwen	1680	
Amariah	Drewet	1686	
Mary	Dyer	1658	
Richard	Farnsworth	1666	
Sarah	Featherstone	1688	
Judith	Fell	1682	24
Thomas	Forster	1660	
George	Fox	1690	66
Joseph	Fuller	?	25
Elizabeth	Furley	1669	
George	Gray	1689	
Thomas	Hains	1700	9
Mary	Harris	1668	35
Mordecai	Hearn	?	
Francis	Howgill	1668	
Richard	Hubberthorn	1662	56
Robert	Jeckel	1676	
Jonah	Lawson	1683	14
Wilhelm	Leddra	1660	
Patrick	Levington	1694	60
Robert	Lodge	1690	
Thomas	Loe	1668	
John	Mattern	1680	
Margaret	Molleson	1669	42

Benjamin	Padley	1687	
James	Parnel	?	
Francis	Patchet	1677	
Giulielm Maria	Penn	1693	50
Springet	Penn		21
William	Robinson	1659	

Mary	Samm	1680	12
Barbara	Scaif	1686	15
Mary	Scaif	1686	18
William	Sixsmith	1677	21
Humphrey	Smith	1663	
Andrew	Sowle	1695	67
Marmaduke	Stevenson	1659	
Joan	Vokins	1690	
Ann	Whitehead	1686	
Jane	Whitehead	1674	
Robert	Widders	1686	68

Part 2

Name		Death	Age
Mary	Aldam	1660	
Thomas	Aldam	1660	
William	Allen	1679	63
Elizabeth	Barker	1701	28
Sarah	Beckwith	1691	
Sarah	Brown	1693	83
John	Burnyeat	1690	59
Morgan	Cadwolader	1698	19
Joseph	Coale	1664	14
El'beth	Copperthwaite	1697	
John	Crook	1699	82
William	Dewsbury	1688	
William	Garton	1701	66
Elizabeth	Harwan	1698	28
George	Harrison	1656	26
Henry	Haydock	1688	33
Alexander	Jaffray	1673	59
Thomas	Jannay	1696	63
Joan	Kellam	1681	
Margaret	Kellam	1672	
Thomas	Lloyd	1694	45
Charles	Marshall	1698	71
James	Martyn	1691	
Ruth	Middleton	1701	11
Margaret	Mollineux	1695	44
Elizabeth	Moss	1702	39
Charles	Ormston	1684	
John	Ormston	1682	20
Mary	Padley	1695	28
Sarah	Padley	1699	34
Thomas	Robinson	1698	73
Thomas (2nd)	Robinson	1678	23
Richard	Sample	1680	
William	Simpson	1689	
Stephen	Smith	1678	55
William	Smith	1672	
Ann	Staploe	1700	14
John	Steel	1680	

Henry	Stout	1695	65
Andrew	Taylor	1698	55
William	Walker	1694	
Robert	Wardel	1696	
Grace	Watson	1688	19
Mary	Watson	1694	
William	Wilson	1682	

Hannah	Turner	1705	19
William	Turner	1704	61
Richard	Vokins	1696	
Thomas	Vokins	1683	
Elizabeth	Whiddon	1693	
Elizabeth	Wills	1687	12
Thomas	Wresle	1704	

Part 3

Isaac	Alexander	1705	
Richard	Andrews		21
James	B(r)aines	1705	51
Robert	Barclay	1690	42
Eleanor	Barcroft	1678	19
James	Blackhouse	1697	20
Francis	Blaikling	1704	73
John	Blaikling	1705	79
John	Bowron	1704	77
Joshua	Bunion	1696	40
Ann	Camm	1705	79
Eleanor	Cannings		73
William	Captain	1672	
Priscilla	Cotton	1664	
Priscilla	Cuthbert	1701	14
Tacey	Davis	1705	90
Mercy	Emes	1697	
Peter	Fletcher	1698	30
Abraham	Fuller	1694	
Thomas	Gettos	1682	
William	Gibson	1684	55
Roger	Gill	1699	34
Thomas	Gilpin	1702	80
Andrew	Graham	1704	62
Hays	Hamilton	1697	12
Mercy	Johnson	1704	34
Sarah	Kirkbride	1705	29
Edward	Parker	1667	50
Richard	Pike	1668	41
Henry	Pontyn/Pontin	?1690s	67
Priscilla	Richards	1704	24
Hugh	Roberts	1702	
Deborah	Sandham	1695	
Robert	Sandham	1675	
Reuben	Saterthwaite		26
William	Smith	1701	79
hugh	Stamper	1676	
Margaret	Thompson	1688	
Thomas	Thompson	1704	73
Sarah	Thompson	1702	19
Thomas	Upsher	1704	32

Additional sources

Volume 4: edited by John Field, pub 1711
Volume 5: ditto, published 1717

Vol 4		
William Carlisle	1707	68
William Stovey	1705	
John Tomkins	1706	43

Vol 5		
Deborah Bell	1738	49